A Winning Combination

A Winning Combination

The History of Eastern Woodworkers,
Eastern Contracting and Eastern Manufacturing

by Jaye Mingo

LANCELOT PRESS
HANTSPORT, NOVA SCOTIA

DBN: 1335137

HD
9715
.C34
E28
1995

ISBN 0-88999-565-6

Copyright © 1995 Faye E. Mingo

ILLUSTRATION CREDITS
The Mingo Family archives have provided
the illustrations unless otherwise noted.

The author wishes to thank
Ralph Dale, Gander Regional Library Headquarters, Gander,
    Newfoundland
Greg Seaward, *Gander Beacon*, Gander, Newfoundland
Valda Bowe and Ian Blackmore of the North Atlantic Aviation
    Museum, Gander, Newfoundand
Susan Hauer

Published 1995

LANCELOT PRESS LIMITED, Hantsport, Nova Scotia.
Office and production facilities situated on Highway No. 1,
1/2 mile east of Hantsport.

MAILING ADDRESS:
P.O. Box 425, Hantsport, N.S. B0P 1P0

ACKNOWLEDGEMENT: This book has been published with the
assistance of the Canada Council and the Nova Scotia
Department of Education, Cultural Affairs Division.

To Robert O'Neil

Contents

Illustrations

Preface

arold, Ernest and Dudley Mingo and their friend and partner, Bill MacLean, owned and operated Eastern Woodworkers, Eastern Contracting and Eastern Manufacturing during a period spanning four decades, from the late 1930s to the early 1970s. In 1956, Eastern (as the companies became known) employed 1,032 people and thousands more indirectly from head offices in New Glasgow, Nova Scotia. A newspaper article in 1958 described Eastern as "one of the best known of its kind in the country."

In a speech given to the Rotary Club in New Glasgow in 1961, Ernest Mingo stated that from 1951 to 1961, Eastern completed $34 million worth of contracts; its payroll was $4,292,000 and $4 million worth of logs and lumber were purchased locally creating further employment in the province. From other local suppliers, Eastern purchased $1.25 million worth of goods. Eighty percent of the construction of the airport town of Gander, Newfoundland, during the 1950s, and a whole new construction town to support the massive hydro project at Lake Jeneen, in northern Québec, were only two of the major contracts Eastern completed. Schools, churches, shopping centres, government buildings, houses, rinks, factories, hospitals and much more were built by Eastern in every corner of the Atlantic provinces and sometimes abroad as well. A list of Eastern's projects is provided in the Appendix.

As the daughter of Dudley Mingo, I remember the bustle of the plant yards and construction sites of the various companies, with hundreds of men busily going about their jobs to make a living. The yards and sites were noisy. Buzzing saws, roars of truck engines, clanging forklifts and straddle carriers, the swoosh of steam from the mill boiler, hammers rhythmically pounding, lumber slamming one on the other and orders being shouted were constant sounds at Eastern. Beyond the noise, a sweet smell of productivity permeated the air from the newly sawn lumber and wood chips.

The main plant occupying eighteen acres on Brother Street in New Glasgow was a going concern. Everyone seemed to know Eastern, the Mingo brothers, their partner, Bill MacLean, and what they were doing. When all of Eastern's operations closed in 1971, the public interest and notoriety became as silent as the grass now growing in the breeze where the main plant once stood.

During my childhood, although privy to many business maneuvers, I did not appreciate the enormity of what my family was doing at the time. Back then, Eastern was simply where my father worked. Until all the operations shut down, the public accolades waned and the privileges of financial security disappeared, I had not realized what the ramifications of the closure would be, not only to my family, but also to me. When Eastern folded I was twenty-two, married to an architect and heading on my own path in life. I wasn't really concerned about what had caused Eastern to shut down, only how its closure would affect my parents.

Within a few short years, however, when I was no longer able to rely on loans and the usual perks available to the daughter of an owner of one of the largest industries in Atlantic Canada, when I saw my parents' lifestyle change over time from one of privilege and security to one of struggle and isolation, my curiosity was stirred. I wanted to know more about my family: why my father and his brothers, farm boys, became so ambitious; how they got started; what they did to make their business so successful and why their huge industry vanished off the face of the earth.

By 1979, I started to do my own research simply to put something together in a scrapbook to give my father for Christmas. As I interviewed my father and uncles, looked through newspapers at the archives and found photographs, I recognized, for the first time, Eastern's enormous scope — the extent to which it had penetrated every aspect of the construction industry in eastern Canada — dry kilns, cabinetmaking, metal workshop, lumber mill, supply stores, the prefabrication industry, mobile and sectional home industries, development and contracting.

While flipping through old newspapers, I was delighted to learn Eastern had been responsible for many firsts in Atlantic Canada: one of the only two storey prefabricated wood houses manufactured anywhere in the world; some of the first trailers, sectional and mobile homes produced in eastern Canada; and the first straddle carrier (used to move and position heavy loads of lumber) east of British Columbia, which Harold Mingo had designed and assembled in 1951. Eastern had also provided most of the prefab and wartime housing manufactured and assembled in the Maritime provinces.

In retrospect, I am glad I did gather what information I could about Eastern Woodworkers and its subsidiaries. Shortly after I had compiled my scrapbook, the offices of Eastern burned to the ground destroying most of the company's records and photographs. And since then two of the principals of this story have died.

Now, fifteen years later, I believe the history of Eastern, representing an important part of Atlantic Canada's growth and development, is one well worth sharing with others. The story of how these farm boys started with a converted henhouse, made their company with its subsidiaries one of the best known construction and manufacturing industries in the country and then were forced out of business, is a study of family influences, individual talents, hard work, ingenuity, sacrifice, risks and, in some instances, intrigue and fate.

The largest part of Eastern's history is about the Mingo brothers. Harold, Dudley and Ernest Mingo not only owned, but also operated Eastern with their partner, Bill MacLean, and later, with the help of their youngest brother, Carl, who joined them as their purchasing manager several years after the brothers had formed their partnership. I do, however, concentrate specifically on the three older Mingo brothers, who started, operated and owned controlling interest in Eastern.

For me, the journey in writing this book has taken me back to previous generations to reveal some of the motivations that drove these farm boys to do well. I include their family background as a means of putting their lives, personalities and work into perspective. I try to unravel the conditions of their partnership, their business deals and successes, and to shed some light on the circumstances which lead to the closure of Eastern.

I would like to thank Margie (MacLean) MacDonald, Lillian (MacLean) Elliott, Sandra (Mingo) Soosaar and particularly my father, Dudley Mingo, and my uncle, Ernest Mingo, for their help in gathering information for this book. I also wish to thank, posthumously, my uncles Harold and Carl Mingo.

Not Cut Out to be Farmers
1700-1900

*C*onsidering the Mingo brothers created one of the largest industries in Atlantic Canada, it might seem strange that they were brought up on a farm near the Northumberland Shore of Nova Scotia where opportunities for growth, education and development were limited. Where did they get their tremendous drive and ambition which took them from the dark desolation of rural life to the top of their profession in all corners of the Atlantic provinces? And why did they choose the construction industry to forge their mark and not some other enterprise? Well, a good deal of what drove these farm boys, Harold, Dudley, and Ernie Mingo, was (as with most of us) the life and attitudes of their parents, as well as who their ancestors were and what skills they had to give the boys.

When looking at their heritage, it comes as no surprise that the Mingo brothers would choose work in the construction industry. They came from a long line of carpenters and entrepreneurs who thought there was more to life than farming. Said to have been well educated soldiers and artisans with musical talents from Montbeliard, France, the Mingos' ancestors were trained by the Swiss, had German and French influences in their lives and were well enough informed to be able to question the authority of the Roman Church.

The early Mingos, along with all those who had converted to Protestantism in Montbeliard, became known as Huguenots. They worshipped freely in the region under the Edit of Nantes of 1598 until it was revoked in 1685. Then their lives became miserable as they attempted to protect themselves and their faith with little more than sticks and stones. Their churches, schools and homes were burned and many Huguenots were killed. Most who survived fled France and journeyed to the New World.

Christopher Mingo, the Mingos' great-great-great-great-great-grandfather, and his brother are said to have escaped from France in the early 1700s and settled in Philadelphia, where, as entrepreneurs, they set up a foundry for making pots and pans. Apparently the brothers must have had considerable skills in finish carpentry work too, because they taught their successive offspring the ornate and intricate woodworking traditional to their homeland.

Business trading, however, was their first love and their most convenient markets were in the English colonies (now known as the United States) and the French colonies (now known as Canada). At the time there was no love lost between the two regions. Trading was difficult. But, because Christopher's son, John, spoke French, he was able to travel to the French colonies often with his son, Matthew. Posing as fishermen, John and Matthew traded pots and pans with natives in the Atlantic area in exchange for furs, often staying in Halifax to work as bookkeepers until sailing to Holland to sell their traded goods.

Some Mingos eventually settled in Nova Scotia. Matthew knew Colonel DesBarres (1721-1824), a Swiss engineer, also from Montbeliard. DesBarres, who would become one of Nova Scotia's most famous historical figures, owned thousands of acres of land on Nova Scotia's Northumberland shore extending from the River John area to Tatamagouche. The British government gave the land to DesBarres, but he was still greatly in debt, so Matthew loaned him money. To repay him, DesBarres gave Matthew a parcel of land from his grant. Matthew's three sons, John, George and David, were to settle this land but did not, and as a result lost their grant. Matthew's son, George (1772-1855), however, came to Nova Scotia with Matthew in 1809, and decided to stay. In 1814 he bought a parcel of land in Middleton on the back road from River John to Tatamagouche, two and a half miles from Denmark and four and a half miles from Tatamagouche.

The land was and still is a gentle area of the province with rolling hills, rich red farming soil, the warmest waters north of the Carolinas and plentiful game and fishing. To this day, the region between Tatamagouche and River John on or near the Northumberland Strait is largely unspoiled and undeveloped except for scattered cottages along its shores. With little effort, one can imagine how people lived one or two hundred years ago despite the wires for electricity and the paved roads which now exist. Most of the farm houses are as old as the first settlers. Some of their descendants still live in them and, incongruent with the Mingo brothers' ambitions, the area has an easy pace of living. Healthy eighty- or ninety-year-olds can often be seen walking the roads or baling hay in the sunshine of the fields and meadows.

George's land was located in a sheltered area about a mile inland from the Strait. Despite the hardship of clearing the forests to make way for crops and grazing lands, it was fairly easy to farm because the soil was rich and productive. But, like his ancestors who were business people with musical talents and skilled with their hands,

Carpenter George Mingo (1839-1928) and Kate Mingo (1844-1930), the Mingo brothers' paternal grandparents.

George preferred woodworking to farming. He taught the traditional intricate and ornate finish carpentry to his son, Charles (1806-1894), who in turn passed the family skills on to his son, George. As a matter of fact, George became known as Carpenter George in the Northumberland area.

Born in 1839, Carpenter George, a jolly, rotund, good-natured man, was very religious and gave readings from the Scriptures every Sunday morning at the breakfast table. The grandfather of the Mingo brothers, George married his cousin, Kate (born 1844), and in 1860 built a house and carpentry shop on a part of his grandfather's property. The buildings still stand much as they did when first constructed over 130 years ago. Only one owner outside the Mingo family has lived on the property and he is still there today.

Carpenter George, like his forbearers, wasn't satisfied to farm exclusively, so he spent most of his time building houses, barns and the church in Middleton for the folks in the area. He and Kate had many children, eleven in all: three boys and eight girls but, unfortunately, both their eldest sons died young, leaving Allison, their second youngest child (and father of the Mingo brothers) to be their only surviving son.

Born in March 1883, Allison naturally learned the carpentry trade from his father. He was even less enamoured with farm life than his ancestors and, as soon as he could, went to Campbellton, New Brunswick, to help rebuild the town after it had burned down. Rather than return to the farm after leaving Campbellton, Allison instead began work as a finish carpenter on mahogany Pullman cars for the Transcolonial Railway in Amherst, Nova Scotia. His foreman, Ernest Chambers, introduced him to his wife, Jamima Langille Chambers, and their daughter, Ella Mae (born December 1890 and mother of the Mingo brothers).

Ernest Chambers had also been born in the Brule-Tatamagouche-River John area near the Mingos and was a descendant of a Chambers brought out by Wellwood Waugh, the manager of the large grant of land the British government had given Colonel DesBarres. The original Chambers was the first freehold land owner in the area. A point of land across the bay from Tatamagouche is named Chambers Point after him.

Jamima Langille, too, was a descendant of those settlers Colonel DesBarres had brought out to farm the lands he owned. The Langilles, along with Tattries, Patriquins, Jodreys and others were Huguenots from the same Duchy adjacent to and part of Switzerland, at the

Ernest Chambers, the Mingo brothers' maternal grandfather.

time called Montbeliard, where DesBarres and the Mingo ancestors had lived.

Before the turn of the century and after several of their children had been born, Ernest and Jamima moved from the Brule area to Amherst, where Ernest went to work as a carpenter and later a foreman. So, the Mingo brothers came from a long line of finish carpenters on both sides of the family.

Ernest was a very proud and ambitious man. His daughter,

Sadie, born in 1893, a sister to Ella Mae and still living, has said their father was so proud he insisted on building the largest house on the street where they lived in Amherst. After he worked on the Pullman cars, Ernest joined the army as a prison guard in Amherst during the First World War when his son, Charles, was drafted and sent overseas to fight. Ernest, a feisty headstrong man who wasn't afraid to stand up for what he believed, apparently swore if Charles did not come back alive from the war, he would volunteer for active duty, go overseas and kill as many of the enemy as he could himself.

Ernest's daughter, Ella Mae was very much like her father: headstrong, proud, feisty and protective of her family. After she finished high school in Amherst, Ella Mae went to business school to take bookkeeping. An excellent seamstress, Ella Mae was very ambitious and conscious of social status. She dreamed of living a dignified, refined life in Amherst where she would one day open her own tailoring shop for all the best dressed ladies and gentlemen of the town.

But her dreams were never to be realized. Ella Mae Chambers married Allison Mingo in 1909 when he was twenty-seven and she nineteen. They settled in Amherst but the times and circumstances soon forced Allison and Ella Mae to leave the bright lights of Amherst to live at the family farm on the back road leading from River John to Tatamagouche. The move, and particularly farm life, were to prove disastrous for Ella Mae, which is precisely why the Mingos became so ambitious: they never really felt they belonged on a farm any more than their mother did. The lure of town called to them just as it had called to her. And their ancestors' trade was the most logical means to seek the fortune their mother was never able to attain herself.

*Allison Mingo (1883-1944) and Ella Mae Chambers Mingo
(1890-1930), the Mingo brothers' parents in their wedding
portrait of 1909.*

Life on the Farm
1915-1930

*S*enior citizens homes did not exist in Allison and Ella Mae's day. Back then, parents worked hard and children usually helped them live their lives out in their own homes. Because Allison was the only living son, custom and duty pointed the finger at him to care for his parents in their old age. That he was doing quite well on the mahogany Pullman cars in Amherst and his wife still had dreams of opening her tailoring shop in town did not matter. Nor did the fact that they had already been living in Amherst for six years since their marriage and had three children: Harold was born in 1911, Louise in 1913, and Dudley in 1914. The times dictated they must eventually leave town to help Allison's parents on the farm.

Allison and Ella Mae quite naturally fought the move because it would mean great sacrifices on their part and a real dent in the futures of their children. But by 1915, the old folks, Carpenter George and Kate, who were in their mid-seventies and finding life harder to handle alone, needed Allison to help them do the chores and chop the thirty cord of wood required to heat their seven bedroom farmhouse. When Allison and Ella Mae seemed reluctant to move, George and Kate pressured Allison. They hired a lawyer to draw up a new deed officially turning the farm over to their son. Allison knew his parents were frugal and poor. For them to have hired a lawyer meant they were serious about needing him. He could not deny them help any longer. Neither could Ella Mae, even though she was miserable about going to the farm. She was too proud to be a farm wife, but she didn't have much choice: she had to follow her husband.

Had Ella Mae and Allison stayed in Amherst, no doubt life would have turned out much differently for them and their children, especially their sons. Perhaps the boys would have carried on as carpenters as the men in their family had done for generations before them. Perhaps they would have gone into business together and been fairly ambitious anyway. But the fact that Allison, Ella Mae and their children were forced to leave Amherst for a farm on the back road to River John made the difference.

In the autumn of 1915, Allison, tall, slim, and handsome with refined features, and Ella Mae, a fine looking woman with noble carriage and dark features, reluctantly packed up their three children and moved to the farm, perhaps not without some hope. Allison and Ella Mae expected the old folks, given their ages, to pass on soon, which would mean they could be back in Amherst before too long. Carpenter George and Kate, however, lived long lives.

So Ella Mae, a proud, dignified and ambitious woman with dreams, moved from a bustling town into someone else's home, a farmhouse to boot, in an area where there were no street lights, sidewalks, stores, cars, industries or proper schools. And her mother-in-law made sure her citified daughter-in-law understood, without a doubt, that the farm would never be her home no matter how much

The Mingo farm on the Waugh's River Road, Pictou County, Nova Scotia. Carpenter George Mingo built the house and carpenter's shop (left) in 1860.

help might be needed. As a result, the tension between Kate and Ella Mae grew, and directly or indirectly spilled over onto the children.

Sometimes Kate treated Ella Mae as if she didn't exist. If, for instance, Ella Mae were cooking something on the stove for her brood, which grew from three to seven (Ernest was born in 1917, Grace was born in 1919, Marion in 1921 and Carl in 1923), Kate would take Ella Mae's cast-iron pot off the wood stove to replace it with her own.

Arguments often developed between the two women and Allison wasn't much help. As the baby of the family and the only surviving son, Allison, a non-smoker, non-drinker and hard worker, was the apple of his mother's eye. Somehow Kate could always manage to get Allison on her side. Only Ella Mae's father-in-law, Carpenter George, could smooth out Kate's fury. He would simply have to say: "Now Mother, leave things be." And Kate would for a time, much to Ella Mae's relief.

Unlike others in the area who were content to stay at home on the farm, Ella Mae and Allison visited Amherst with their children as often as they could. Being sensitive to her social standing, Ella Mae, with a perfectionist's eye to the quality of cloth and its tailoring, made suits and dresses for her children to wear to make sure there wasn't a trace of the country in them when they were in town. And this attitude rubbed off. Even on the farm, dressing well became second nature to the children and, later, their panache for style often put them at an advantage in their business dealings. As Dudley would say, "We were always dressed for whomever walked in the front door, no matter whom it might be — supposing it might have been the premier or the prime minister."

Trying to keep some contact with life in Amherst, however, was not easy for either Allison or Ella Mae. Their trips were expensive and they both had to work hard to support them. Allison got up at five o'clock in the morning to feed the horse, get his breakfast, drive the horse and buggy four or five miles to where there was work, drop them off at the stable, walk a mile or so to the work site to be there by seven o'clock in the morning, work ten hours a day six days a week doing carpentry work, and return home at seven o'clock at night to do farm chores. Only brief periods during the winters provided some respite from this grind. But even in the winter Allison usually spent long hours in the carpentry shop building advance orders of windows, doors, and other items of millwork for customers to use when weather permitted in the spring. Whatever Allison and Ella Mae could do to earn extra money to escape the dark desolation of the farm to go to the bright lights of Amherst once or twice a year, they did.

Ella Mae, rather than pay an outsider to pull the turnips on the farm, would contract from her own husband to do it herself. Apparently, she could pull an acre of turnips faster than any man. She probably had to be fast in order to accomplish all that was required of her in the run of a day: up at five o'clock in the morning with Allison, Ella Mae helped with the farm work, baked three loaves of bread and two dozen rolls every morning ("Mother bought ninety-eight pounds of flour a week," Harold said), cooked three meals a day for eleven people, did the housework, painted and wallpapered whenever necessary, made most of the children's clothing, reared them and took in sewing to help earn extra money for their trips. Her visits to Amherst kept her in touch with a way of life she wanted and Carpenter George helped calm her nerves when arguments broke out between Ella Mae and her mother-in-law.

With parents as hard-working as theirs, the Mingo children quite naturally became hard workers too. For one thing, Allison and Ella Mae expected their children to pitch in and to manage their own money at an early age. From the money they earned doing work on the farm, the children were required to pay their own expenses. "This responsibility," Ernie says, "inspired us to want to earn more money, so we often took on chores for the neighbours to add to our incomes."

The farm was a temporary place to live, however, and all the children knew it. Especially tuned in to their mother, they knew real life belonged in Amherst or some other large centre, not on the farm. Whatever glimmer of hope there was to get them off the farm, they took. For instance, when Dudley and Ernie visited their cousins in Amherst, they borrowed books written by Frank Merriwell, the great baseball player. Dudley and Ernie relished these books about farm boys who went to the city and did well. They would pretend to be boys in the stories and go out into the yard with their cousins and their friends to play ball. Athletic anyway — Dudley was a great runner and Ernie a great pole jumper (these activities became characteristics of their business dealings later on) — the boys took their games seriously. "Baseball, we thought, might be one way we could get off the farm," says Dudley.

One of the reasons the children tuned in so well to their mother and how she felt about the farm was because Ella Mae was a compassionate and loving mother who lived for her children. Feisty, protective and concerned about each of them, she often defended them against others. Once, for instance, when a larger boy choked Harold to the point of making him pass out, Ella Mae grabbed Ernie by the hand, marched to the neighbour's house to confront the boy and his parents and declared in no uncertain terms: "If you ever touch one of my children again, you'll have to deal with me."

Ernie remembers the incident well and adds, "Father wasn't like that. He'd never have done that." Allison was much too severe a disciplinarian himself to defend one of his children. He would more than likely want to know what Harold had done to cause the boy to choke him in the first place and not care that the punishment he had received was way out of line. Allison was often way out of line himself with the discipline he enforced on some of the children.

Dudley remembers a time when Harold, four years older than he, convinced him to play hooky, something Harold was often want to do when it came to responsibilities even later in life. Harold made Dudley swear that if they were caught he would say they had left school at the regular time. A neighbour saw the two boys and told their father. Allison took each of the boys aside individually, Harold first, who told his father the truth and managed to get out of being punished, and then Dudley, who did as his brother instructed him to do, lied and received a beating because of it. Dudley was a little more than sore at Harold for that one but he was not the only one their father would beat. Allison would beat Harold the most of all the children, perhaps because he was the oldest. "Harold would zigzag all over the yard trying to get away from Father," Dudley says, "but Father was always too fast for him. Pitiful, really," he adds sadly.

By the time Harold was eleven, Allison had sciatic rheumatism and wasn't able to do both the farm work and the carpentry, so Harold had to take over most of the farm chores. The shortest of the Mingo brothers, Harold was so young to be doing the work he had to make steps for himself to reach the horse to harness it. He plowed, sowed and hoed the fields and took care of the animals. Yet Harold assumed the tasks with the maturity of someone much older, getting up at dawn, working the farm, walking two miles to school, two miles back, and working the farm again. Perhaps, having so much responsibility at such a young age was too much for Harold. Something had to give and, unfortunately, it was school.

But Harold did not mind. He didn't like school at all and Ernie, six years younger than Harold, recalls the day Harold persuaded him to play hooky with him. "It was a bitterly cold winter day," Ernie says. "There was a vacant logging camp on the property on the way to school so we made our shelter there for the whole day. I nearly froze to death," he says, then chuckles, "Needless to say, I never played hooky from school again."

The cold didn't bother Harold, though. He would rather have frozen to death than spend a day in school. Shy and very much a loner, perhaps Harold had problems with school because his father never really understood him. Allison expected a lot from Harold and Harold resented

Allison because of it. Unlike Dudley and Ernie who loved to play baseball and hockey, go to dances and parties and read, Harold went off by himself to tinker in the carpentry shop.

Harold loved nothing better than to work with his hands, to take machines apart, put them back together again and try to come up with a new way of making something. Eddie Mingo, Harold's cousin, taught him whatever he knew about machines but Allison never understood Harold's need to experiment. If Harold did try to take a machine apart and put it back together again to see how it worked, he more often than not was given a real pounding from his father for doing so.

Once Harold took the mowing machine apart and didn't replace one of its parts correctly. When Allison tried to mow the hay and the machine wouldn't work, one could understand that he would be pretty upset. But Allison never really recognized the talent Harold had. He never encouraged Harold. Instead, Allison went after Harold, yelling at him that his tinkering with machines was a waste of time. What Allison never knew was that years later when Harold was to build his own sawmill, he remembered how the mowing machine was constructed. He added on a few parts to the slab slasher which cut firewood, making it automatic, the only one of its kind at the time.

Harold left school at fourteen, a common occurrence back then. Some teachers were not very good — often young and impatient — with barely more than a high school education themselves. Harold's quick mind became easily bored in the one room school, where he learned whatever he could, then sat listening to lessons from other grades long past the time he had finished his own work. Miss Helen Douglas was the only teacher who captured Harold's attention. She was a very gentle woman, never raising her voice and had the ability to make her students understand and learn. When Harold discovered she would not be returning, he quit school. He had only completed grade five, which is really quite amazing considering that Harold would prove to be a genius in mechanics and inventing later in life.

Harold knew he was smart. And he didn't have to have someone to tell him so. "I could always take care of myself," he once said. But not having much of an education did create problems for him. "I felt a little backward at times," he remarked, "and had trouble talking to people." Rarely speaking up, Harold often mumbled, dragging his voice self-consciously when he did.

Yet, there was a presence about Harold which made people feel as if he were always in control. Certainly Harold was an authority figure to his two younger brothers when he dominated the farm. And his ability to be closed-mouthed about himself often put him in a position of power. Harold said little, unnerving others, in turn making them talk about themselves. The result was, Harold gleaned information he needed or could use. And just as he had been able to get Dudley to lie for him or to get Ernie to skip school with him, Harold was shrewd enough to get people on his side, to get them to do what he wanted and to keep his secrets for him.

After Harold left school, he worked at the sawmill in Denmark and in the woods during the winter. When he worked at carpentry, Harold showed enormous patience with himself, never getting frustrated or angry if he made mistakes, simply seeing them as learning experiences, correcting them and doing a better job the next time. He was a perfectionist with his woodcraft and machine work, much as his mother was with her tailoring. As a child, Harold had even made a motorbike out of his bicycle by buying an engine from someone who could not get it to work. Convincing a neighbour to put money up for the motor in exchange for labour, Harold compared his engine to one in a magazine picture and realized the carburetor had been put in upside down. He soon fixed that, attached it to his bike and was off, scaring all the horses around.

By 1928, thirteen years after Allison had moved his family to the farm, the situation between Kate and Ella Mae showed no signs of improvement. One afternoon that year, Allison and Ella Mae took Kate and all the children, except Dudley and Ernie, visiting in a new touring "Starcar" a friend owned. Carpenter George, who had kept some semblance of peace between his wife and daughter-in-law over the years, stayed home with his grandsons.

Eighty-nine at the time and in the habit of not lacing his high black boots, George decided to go to the carpentry shop to get kindling for the stove upstairs. After he had gathered the sticks, George stepped down the two stairs from the shop and tripped over his untied lace. Dudley, thirteen, happened to be looking towards his grandfather as George stumbled feebly down the steps, collapsing on the ground with the guilty boot lying beside him.

Hollering to him, Dudley tried to help his grandfather but realized George was not breathing properly. Very fond of him, Dudley knew how much George meant to his mother, too. In a panic, he grabbed his bicycle and pumped as fast as he could a half a mile down the road to the Camerons' house to get help.

When he got there, Dudley was so upset he could not get the right words out. Cameron thought the Mingo house must be on fire because only recently there had been two fires along their road. Snatching Dudley's bike from him, Cameron tore off to the Mingos with Dudley running at full speed behind him. There wasn't a fire of course, but by the time they arrived back at the Mingo farm, there was nothing Cameron could do for George. He was already dead. Cameron did, however, realize a person had to be laid out as soon as possible — within two hours before rigor mortis set in — so he yelled at Dudley to get to Eddie Mingo's place as quickly as possible because Eddie knew what to do.

"I was already really upset about Grandfather's death," Dudley recalls. "I was pumping as hard as I could through a shortcut in the woods when a deer jumped into my path, startling me out of my wits. I slammed on my brakes, caught my breath, then continued on to Eddie's house."

Back at the house, Eddie laid George out on a sheathing storm door between two chairs in the living room until he could place him on boards in his bed to keep his body straight. Then the rest of the family was notified of George's death and they returned to the farm. Eddie took George to the bedroom to prepare him but until he had finished, none of the children was allowed in the room. They knew the windows had to be kept open and ice tubs kept fresh around grandfather's bed.

Now there was little peace left at the farm for Ella Mae. The battles between her and Kate became more unbearable. Ella Mae needed an escape. Since people of Tatamagouche had grown to respect her as an excellent seamstress and were demanding more and more of her time, Ella Mae, even though pregnant with her youngest and eighth child, Kathleen, opened a shop in Tatamagouche in the upstairs section of a local store. Her tailoring kept her busy, away from Kate, and the money went towards more trips to her beloved Amherst for her family.

By now, even though Harold did odd jobs in carpentry with his father around the area, he resented Allison so much he refused to work the farm anymore. In fact, Harold actually worked other people's farms for free rather than farm his father's. As a result, Dudley, at fourteen, became, as he would say himself, "supreme boss" of the farm.

Before he took over the farm, Dudley had the contract as janitor of the school for thirty dollars a year. In blizzards or sunshine, Dudley collected kindling at the farm each morning, walked the two miles to school before anyone else arrived, lit the potbelly coal stove, kept it going and at the end of the day, swept the floors and dusted the desks.

Sometimes, his younger brother, Ernie, helped him and after school they would set off to a neighbour's farm to do the barn work there — watering the horses, cleaning out the manure and hauling down the hay. Getting ten cents a day for doing the neighbour's barn work, Dudley and Ernie decided then and there that one day they would be their own bosses and become millionaires.

A girl outbid Dudley for the janitor's job when he was fourteen and he decided the job wasn't worth it to him anymore even though the school told him it could still be his. Besides, his father needed him to do the work on the farm now that Harold was no longer willing to do it.

As many children are, Dudley was intimidated by his older sibling. He knew he lacked the patience Harold had for working with his hands. If Harold was a perfectionist, Dudley was even more so. If he was working on something that didn't turn out exactly right, he would, likely as not, throw the thing against the wall, smashing it. Dudley was more interested in observing other people's work and pointing out their flaws to them so they could improve the next time, than actually doing the work himself. At the time, he did not realize this was quite a talent. But it was.

Dudley was good with people, a great communicator and organizer, and he had no problem whatsoever in telling others what to do. His mind was practical and efficient and he could see solutions to problems quicker than most. He did not want to spend hours tinkering with machines or working with wood. He wanted to walk ahead of the crowd and get them to follow him. He had a genius for doing this as a boy working on the farm or organizing ball games or dances, and later in life he would command hundreds of men. In the meantime, he understood his duties on the farm, got on much better with his father than Harold ever did and took on the work with maturity and authority. Yet he too longed to get off the farm. In a strange twist of fate, Dudley had actually been born on the farm even though he lived his first year in Amherst. While visiting from Amherst when pregnant with him, Ella Mae had gone into labour at the farm. This was and always would be a source of aggravation: the farm was not the place to have been born.

Dudley's name was also much cause for consternation. Taken from the last name of the midwife who guided Ella Mae through her delivery, the name Dudley was not one he would have chosen. Even his grandparents, Kate and George, insisted on calling Dudley "Tom" which didn't help endear them to his mother who had named him.

The arguments between his grandmother and his mother and the fact that his father always seemed to take his grandmother's side, made Dudley dislike the farm even more. Sensitive to his mother's struggles on the farm, Dudley hated the fact that Ella Mae had to work so hard and was not able to live in Amherst. He would lie in bed dreaming of the day when he would be big enough and strong enough to take his mother away to a place where life would be much easier for her. He loved his mother, as all the children did, and could see that the pace she was keeping was running her into the ground.

Often, Ella Mae would be on her hands and knees scrubbing the floor — after she had baked and made breakfast for her brood — when the train whistle would blow behind the house. Then, she would snatch her things to run off to the siding to catch the train to Tatamagouche. Harold has said that while he was still on the farm his mother would pay him a few pennies to stay up with her until three or four o'clock in the morning while she sewed orders for customers by oil lamp. Understandably, when her nerves started to fray she did not like to be up alone. Still, she would get up the next morning to do it all over again because now she lived for her children. Her dreams had not come true so she worked herself into a frenzy to make sure that her children's would.

One Christmas Eve, Ella Mae arrived back at the farm from Tatamagouche by train at five o'clock and realized she had left the children's Christmas gifts for the next day back at the shop. She turned straight around, walked four and a half miles to Tatamagouche in the dark and cold to get the gifts and then walked four and a half miles back home. She would not see her children go without Christmas gifts no matter what the consequences to herself.

With the farm work, the household cleaning, the meals, the baking, the dress shop and having to tend eight children, inevitably Ella Mae's health began to deteriorate. Her nerves were shot. She was losing weight. Her local doctor was treating her but had diagnosed her problem incorrectly, so his treatments were not doing her any good. When she visited her sisters in Amherst in the summer of 1930, she was in such bad shape they immediately sent her to a doctor there. Diagnosed with a hyperactive thyroid, iodine and rest were prescribed for her but Ella Mae refused to rest. By now, fifteen years after arriving on the farm, Ella Mae's nerves were so bad she couldn't even hold a teacup and saucer anymore.

In December of that year, Ella Mae was forced to take the train to Halifax, Nova Scotia, for further tests and an operation at the Victoria General Hospital (VG). Before she left, as she got on the train at the siding, Ella Mae turned to her son, Dudley, as he stood by his father, and said: "You take care of your father, you hear?"

Four weeks after Ella Mae left for Halifax, Ernie, just about to turn fourteen, was walking home from school with his younger sisters and brothers when a neighbour shouted to them as they passed by: "Your mother's dead!" Ernie never forgot the callous way in which the neighbour told him and his younger siblings about their mother's death. For years, he would not believe his mother had died. Until he was sixteen or seventeen, Ernie pretended she was just away somewhere and would be home again soon.

Dudley, sixteen, was at home in the kitchen talking to Owny Mingo when he got the news about his mother's death. "The roars came out of me," he says. "I went into the living room, Owny following me trying to get me to stop but I wouldn't. I couldn't. I went on hollering like that for the rest of the night."

When Ella Mae died, Harold was nineteen, Dudley, sixteen, Ernie, not quite fourteen and Carl was seven. Kathleen, the youngest was two. Ella Mae had just turned forty herself.

Ironically, two weeks after Ella Mae entered the VG, Kate, her rival and nemesis, died of pneumonia at eighty-six. No one had had the heart to tell Ella Mae, since she was dying herself, that the person who had made her life so miserable was gone.

So, within two weeks of each other, in the bone chilling ten degrees below zero (Fahrenheit) temperatures of January, Allison and the children had to bury Kate and then Ella Mae. Allison used his own punt and horses for his mother's funeral. For the mother of his eight children, he hired a fine black carriage with windows and lanterns on either side of it. Drawn by two black, stately horses, with a driver dressed in black, the carriage represented the dignity with which Ella Mae had always wanted to conduct her life. The gesture was the least Allison could do for his wife who had died at far too young an age.

Getting off the Farm
1929-1933

*F*or Harold, Dudley, and Ernie, their mother's early death was inextricably linked to life on the farm. Now more than ever they were determined to get away so they could fulfil ambitions their mother was never able to realize herself. Yet even though none of them was cut out to be a farmer, none was a carpenter either. Harold was more an inventor and mechanic than anything; Dudley, an organizer and problem solver, and Ernie was more interested in the facts and figures of business. Still, they all learned the carpentry trade from their father and with this in common, often talked in their youth about forming a business together one day.

Harold was the first to leave the farm. In 1929, a year or so before his mother died, Harold had ridden his bike to Thorburn, Nova Scotia, to stay with his mother's sister, Margaret. He wanted to take in a dance and to look for a factory job while there.

Harold had learned his mother's lesson well — always look better than the next guy. So despite the shaky economic times of the Great Depression, he had bought himself a suit. Dressed in his new outfit, Harold set off for the factories of nearby New Glasgow, Nova Scotia.

No one was hiring at the time but that didn't stop Harold. He simply hopped on his bike and drove around town to see if there was any construction going on. He saw a house being built and asked the boss, Simon Fraser, of Fraser Mason Fraser (FMF), if he might have a job. He got it, borrowed a good set of tools from his Aunt Margaret's husband and went to work. Within no time, Harold, with considerable resentment from fellow workers, was being paid more than others who had been working over three years at the same job.

Within a year of arriving in New Glasgow, Harold had married Marge MacDonald. He had met Marge one night just before Christmas in 1929. Harold wasn't used to drinking at the time, but a friend had convinced Harold to have a few drinks with him. Harold felt he didn't have money for drinking, and since he wouldn't waste money to pay for his own, couldn't accept offers from others. Harold and his friend had gone downtown to buy toys for their boss's children. So perhaps in the spirit of the season, this night had been an exception.

Leaning his stocky frame against the shop doorway, his hat tilted over his dark eyes and hair, Harold waited as his friend talked to two girls he knew. One of the girls, Marge, asked, "Who's your friend over there?" Soon he and Marge were married.

Not always a happy marriage, the conflicts between Harold and Marge spurred him on to work harder than the average man. Like his mother who avoided conflicts at home by keeping herself busy in her shop at Tatamagouche, Harold avoided domestic clashes and earned extra money working at night to build walk-in coolers in the large basement of the Brother Street house he and Marge rented in New Glasgow.

Meanwhile, the irony of the deaths of his grandmother

and mother within two weeks of each other had never left Dudley. His mother's death deepened his hatred of the farm which had already been imbedded in him when he had to slaughter an animal at fourteen. From that time until he was eighteen, Dudley would not eat meat at all. After that, and throughout the rest of his life, he never ate much meat ever again. This probably accounted for his excellent health despite the fact that he smoked for years.

Never a very religious person in the first place, Dudley did not have much to do with religion after the deaths of his grandfather, grandmother and mother within a two year period, except for social convenience. Instead, he studied people "to see how they worked." He learned to talk to anyone with ease, and with the odd story, endeared himself to them. He worked hard and was determined to get away from the farm for all time.

When he left school in grade ten, Dudley worked at the mill in Denmark where Harold had once worked. He later worked for another sawmill and part of his duties was to haul logs by horse and punt across a frozen lake. The horse had not been shod properly and struggled, slipping across the ice. Dudley told his boss about the horse but was warned not to have it reshod until a stormy day. Well, a stormy day did not come soon enough for Dudley. He could not stand the situation—slipping and sliding all over the ice. This wasn't fair to the horse and it wasn't a very efficient way to work. The job was taking twice as long as it should. Dudley knew the horse had to be reshod right away to save time on labour. So, on a fine day, Dudley rode the horse to the blacksmith's to be reshod. He wanted to show the boss he could take initiative. Unfortunately, the boss didn't see it that way. He caught Dudley disobeying his orders and fired him. If anything, the fact that he was fired made Dudley even more determined to become his own boss one day so he would never again have to "suffer fools" who might be his boss.

Time was extremely important to Dudley. He had an innate sense of its value. All Allison had to do in the morning was click the latch on his bedroom door and Dudley was awake. Usually the first to arrive at an event or on a job, Dudley was an affable character who enjoyed his leisure time as much as his work. Dudley's ability to grasp the juxtaposition of leisure and work — he could not enjoy his leisure without knowing he had done a job well first and he could not enjoy a job unless he knew he would have time for leisure — was the primary reason Dudley was able to become one of the best contractors this country ever had. Later, men who would work for Dudley knew that he expected them to do a job well the first time, in turn freeing them to enjoy their time off. Time was money and realizing this, Dudley made profits wherever he was, working in his own companies or working for others.

But when Dudley was coming of age to work, the Great Depression was in full swing. Even jobs he could have helped his father with around the area were becoming more scarce by the minute. Dudley felt trapped on the farm by the Depression and was forced to snare rabbits to live.

With whatever money he made, Dudley used it to go to Amherst. Going to Amherst then was what going to New York might be today. There was excitement, activity and opportunities for great gatherings. Few people had jobs back then. With whatever was left from their three dollars a week rationing, the majority of the people gathered in the streets to play baseball, make music, dance, and organize church plays. Dudley's visits to Amherst were happy times for him as a teenager and provided momentary escapes from the farm and the Depression.

One unhappy incident in Amherst, however, affected Dudley's life forever. Two boys, both Dudley's age, nineteen, schemed to rob an old lady whose husband owned a store. When the woman opened her door to the boys, one of them hit her with a board so hard it killed her. The boys were caught when they flashed twenty dollar bills around. No one in those days had that kind of money so they were immediately suspected, arrested, convicted of murder and sentenced to hang. Streets were cordoned off in Amherst and a gallows constructed.

Dudley happened to be in Amherst at the time. Since the excitement of the day, believe it or not, was to see the bodies afterwards, he decided to go. They were to be laid out as an example to others.

The hangings sent the chief of police to bed for two weeks, staring at the ceiling for what had been done. For Dudley, the sight of the bloated and disfigured bodies of these boys, his own age, went beyond revulsion. From then on, the result of what may happen to someone who steals had a new and significant meaning. Later, when he owned his own business, Dudley would hesitate to take even a board or brick for his own use. The image of those boys could never be erased from his memory.

Now and again, Dudley went to New Glasgow to help Harold with his extra orders for walk-in coolers. One day in 1935, Harold's boss, Simon Fraser, came to visit while Dudley was there. Fraser asked Dudley what he planned to do for a living and when Dudley said he would take up the carpentry trade, Simon told him that if FMF got a big job that was coming up, he would call Dudley.

Twenty-one in 1936 and back on the farm, Dudley was in the woods with his father cutting trees for firewood when a neighbour came puffing through the fields towards them with a message from Harold saying that Simon Fraser's job had come through and Dudley was to leave for New Glasgow immediately. Dudley put down his saw, looked at his father and said, "This is it. I'm going for all time." He rushed to the house, packed his clothes and was off to the siding to catch the 5 p.m. train.

Grace, his sister, had just returned from Tatamagouche on the train as Dudley was boarding, so he told her he was leaving for good. Well, she started to "hoot and holler" pleading with him not to go. Dudley had kept the family in good cheer with his jokes, his singing and with many family friends he brought home. Grace wanted him to stay but Dudley wanted out of there. He squeezed his sister's arm, boarded the train and never went back to the farm again except for short visits with the family.

Ernie was determined enough, and stubborn enough, to make sure he would get off the farm, become a millionaire and stay that way. Never giving up in an argument, Ernie would keep going until he knew all the why's of everything. Unlike Harold who was six years older or Carl who was seven years younger, Ernie was close to Dudley in age. They had been best friends, slept in the same room, played together, worked together, fought together and sometimes bloodied each other's noses.

One winter day when Ernie had to attend a Boy Scout meeting in Tatamagouche five miles away, he wanted Dudley to do his farm work for him. Dudley refused because he already had enough to do himself. Perhaps naively, Dudley always felt if everyone did his own work, things would turn out all right. Ernie, however, would not take no for an answer. Dudley decided the only thing he could do to get his point across was to punch his brother in the nose. And then the fight was on.

Ernie never won a fist fight with Dudley but he would always give it his best shot. They fought so hard this time that their older sister, Louise, who had taken their mother's place at the farm, stood at the door waving her apron in her hands screaming: "They're killing each other! They're killing each other! Someone stop them!" But there was no stopping Ernie. Before the fight had ended, the snow in the field was flattened, the two brothers were exhausted and Ernie, bloody and all, was still angry with Dudley. Dudley may have won the fight but he had to make a concession to his brother for trying hard. He did Ernie's barn work for him after all.

In the end, Ernie often won out somehow but not without effort. Perhaps because he was younger than Harold and Dudley, Ernie had the opportunity to see their mistakes and avoided making them himself.

Since Ernie was not quite fourteen when his mother died, his Aunt Margaret did what she could to take his mother's place. Ernie was a brilliant student at school with an aptitude in math — so good he was able to take grade one and two in one year and grades seven and eight in another. He was fourteen in grade ten, but unfortunately failed the grade by one subject. "I had to put crops in at the farm that year," Ernie explains, "which took two weeks to do just before exam time."

By the time he was sixteen in 1933, Ernie completed grade eleven and went to live with his Aunt Margaret in Thorburn in order to attend business school in New Glasgow. Now he too had made his break from the farm, a little earlier and perhaps a little smoother than his older brothers had, but he had made the break.

The Early Years of Eastern
1938-1945

*W*hile working for FMF from 1929 to 1937, Harold decided to take correspondence courses to upgrade his math and to learn to be a draftsman. He had become known as one of the best carpenters FMF had ever had and people were becoming aware that he was doing precision work in his basement.

By 1937, Harold's basement was no longer big enough to accommodate the growing orders for walk-in coolers. An old henhouse was located on the property on Brother Street, so Harold rented the building for fifteen dollars a month and quit his job with FMF. His reputation for high quality woodworking soon grew, and encouraged by the demand for his products, Harold converted the old henhouse into a mill for cabinetwork, show cases, refrigerators and small millwork.

Harold was a driven man during this period of his life. He was not happy with his marriage yet he was keenly aware of his responsibilities to see it through. To keep his mind off his personal problems, Harold worked night and day and his efforts were paying dividends. He was a master at inventing new equipment to suit his needs and

The Brother Street henhouse, New Glasgow, Nova Scotia, original site of Eastern Woodworkers, established 1938. Harold G. Mingo converted it to a millwork plant.

was an exceptional craftsman. All of his siblings were extremely proud of Harold. He was setting an example for the males in his family — an example that was very difficult to live up to.

When Harold rented and converted the old henhouse, Jim MacKay was also renting part of the building as an office for his business of collecting garbage for the town of New Glasgow. Jim was more a salesperson than anything, with a good gift of the gab and an aggressive business manner.

By the end of 1938, Harold and Jim began to recognize each other's assets. Jim saw that Harold was doing well in the millwork, had a tremendous ability for inventing new equipment and was gaining a credible reputation in town. Harold was doing well on his own but always felt insecure about his education. He understood that if he were to become even more successful in his business, he would have to have someone to promote his work. Jim seemed the logical sort, being well known in New Glasgow and engaged to the daughter of H.B. MacCulloch, a member of parliament from Nova Scotia. With Harold's expertise and Jim's outgoing manner, they felt they could make a successful business together.

Harold and Jim formed a partnership and called their company Eastern Woodworkers. At the time, there were no thoughts of Harold's younger brothers coming in with them. Dudley was still relatively young, having worked only two years with FMF, and Ernie was still in school.

While Harold was gaining experience in the carpentry trade at FMF and later in his own business, and while Dudley was running the farm and later working for FMF, Ernie was spending most of his time in his room at his Aunt Margaret's house in Thorburn, studying law and accounting and taking pleasure in learning. Only one other person in his business course did as well as Ernie and he was five years older. Both in New Glasgow and Halifax, Ernie had the highest marks in bookkeeping.

After business school, Ernie's first job was with FMF, a company which by now had trust in the abilities of the Mingo brothers. But unlike Harold and Dudley, Ernie's talents did not lie in carpentry. He wanted to be an accountant.

When a job became available at a garage in New Glasgow, in 1936, Ernie took it knowing he would have a better chance of achieving his goal than if he remained doing carpentry work. He knew that he would have to start at the bottom and work his way up. So for ten dollars a week, six dollars of which was taken for room and board, Ernie worked sixteen hours a day, six days a week pumping gas, cleaning the garage, selling goods and managing the books.

During that year, Ernie and Dudley 'bached' together, often going over to Harold and Marge's for Sunday dinners and talking about forming their own business together. As a result, Ernie decided to take a course in drafting at night school and won a certificate for making the most progress in class. But then Ernie obtained a job in Sydney, Nova Scotia, at an auto dealership which put a hold on any idea of working together.

At the dealership, Ernie started in the stockroom and worked his way up. When he heard of a job in Glace Bay, Nova Scotia, as manager of parts for another auto dealership, Ernie applied, and with good recommendations was able to get the job. "I was able to dictate my wages," Ernie says. "I got 2% on parts, thirty dollars a week and 5% on any cars I sold. In one year, I earned over $2,400 which was a lot of money back then."

Meanwhile, for a year or so of Harold and Jim's partnership they had only a verbal agreement between them. With his education in business and law, Ernie knew it was important that Harold get something in writing, so he advised Harold to do something about it right away. Harold was no fool either, despite his lack of education. Because Jim was so well known in New Glasgow and so politically well-connected, Harold felt he should try to find a lawyer from somewhere other than New Glasgow to draw up the documents for their partnership. Since Ernie was in Glace Bay in 1939, Harold asked Ernie to find a lawyer to put him in as secure a position as possible. A lawyer friend of Ernie's drew up the document which stated that neither Jim nor Harold could form his own company while still in a partnership with the other.

The first sizeable millwork order Eastern obtained was for refrigerator parts at a cold storage plant in Canso, Nova Scotia, in the spring of 1939. From this start, work for Eastern expanded to include restaurant furnishings and remodelling. By early 1940, Harold and Jim put a tender in and received a contract for millwork for the Sydney Airport worth $75,000. The job was completed in the spring of 1941. Then they secured a contract for millwork and hangar doors for the Summerside Airport, Prince Edward Island (P.E.I.).

Later in 1941, housing in the New Glasgow area was badly needed, so Harold and Jim turned their attention to that. The first contract for Wartime Housing (which became Central Mortgage and Housing Corporation (CMHC) around 1949-1950) was tendered and Eastern Woodworkers secured an initial contract to prefabricate 250 houses for the car works, steel works and gunnery shop in the Trenton/New Glasgow area. This was Eastern's first large-scale contract.

Working for FMF, Dudley had acquired a great deal of knowledge about the construction industry which Harold could use. Part of the 250 house contract in 1941 included funds to build a new plant to facilitate prefabrication. Harold asked Dudley to come to build the plant. Dudley readily agreed because he believed his brother would give him a far better chance of being his own boss.

Bill MacLean had also been working for FMF as a foreman since 1935. A mutual respect had developed between him and the Mingos, so when Harold needed to hire more employees to look after his growing orders, he naturally asked Bill to come work with him too. Bill had been happy working with FMF, was older than Dudley and had worked as a foreman, so part of the deal to entice Bill to leave his job was a contract for one year, with the stipulation that he might be able to become a partner after the year was up. Bill left FMF but according to Harold, at the end of that first year, Jim refused to allow Bill to become a partner. This must have upset Bill considerably. Not enough, however, for him to leave Eastern. In fact, Bill stayed with the company to the bitter end.

Born in 1909, Bill MacLean was also brought up on a farm several miles east of the Mingos in Scotsburn, Nova Scotia, with his parents, Osborne and Margerite, and his four siblings. Never having liked the farm, Bill was influenced by his mother who had travelled, worked in the States and was director of many church plays in Scotsburn. Like Dudley, Bill was horrified at having to slaughter animals, a job which revolted him so much that he left the farm to attend Pictou Academy. Bill then went out west to Vancouver Tech where he received training as a carpenter. From there, Bill took the harvest train to Swift Current, Saskatchewan, where he worked for several years before his inherent love of family and home country drew him back to Scotsburn. After arriving back on the farm in Scotsburn, Bill married Marion Sutherland from Balmoral Mills, Nova Scotia, and they moved to New Glasgow, where Bill worked for FMF as a carpenter and foreman until going to work for Harold and Jim.

An honourable man, Bill was a jolly person, over-weight, with a good nature. But he did have a bit of a stubborn streak in him, too. "If Bill decided to do something," Ernie says, "he'd do it his way. You couldn't get him to do it any other way. He was a good man, though, and a good estimator, very loyal and very keen to make a profit. Bill watched things very carefully." As a matter of fact, Bill was so meticulous about checking every bit of work to be done that by the '60s the workmen had nicknamed him Chubby Checker.

Dudley and Bill constructed the plant for the 250 houses. The houses were prefabricated and Eastern was to erect them on their sites, which would have been another sizeable contract. Unfortunately, some of the other contractors in the area were getting a little nervous about the rapid success of Eastern Woodworkers. They also wanted to get their fingers in the pie but were unsuccessful. So, having influence with the provincial government, they made such a strong protest that Eastern was not allowed to erect the houses after they had prefabricated them. The 250 houses in stock were eventually sold to a Halifax firm, and a company called Brookfield's — at the time the largest construction and woodworking company around — erected them.

Because Eastern's bid to erect the houses was rejected, C.D. Howe, the minister of supply for Canada at the time, made sure Eastern was able to bid on and receive a contract for 100 houses in Amherst. Howe was somewhat more impartial than the local government, and a friend of H. B. MacCulloch's, who had become Jim's father-in-law by then. "C.D. Howe did an awful lot for Canada," Ernie says. "We were an agricultural country until the war came along. C.D. Howe had plants built all over the country."

Dudley was by now married to Bernice Tattrie, and still only an employee of Harold's. He moved with his wife and their two daughters to Amherst to supervise the construction of the houses. They stayed in Amherst for eight months, than moved back to New Glasgow.

The Second World War was on and with it came incredible opportunities. Pictou, Nova Scotia, a ship-building town, received huge government orders to build warships. People had to be brought in to get them done as quickly as possible. Men, women and children worked twenty-four hours a day to produce a boat every two months. Housing had to be set up for these people, and again through C.D. Howe, Eastern was able to get a major contract for 400 houses.

During this time, Harold remained in New Glasgow supervising millwork and setting up machines for their needs. Jim MacKay also remained in New Glasgow as both office and sales manager. Dudley and Bill drove every day

Wartime housing in Pictou, Nova Scotia circa 1942-43. Eastern prefabricated and erected 400 houses under a contract from Minister of Supply C.D. Howe.

The planer and matcher designed by Harold G. Mingo for Eastern's millwork facilities in New Glasgow, Nova Scotia.

to Pictou in the company's half ton trucks to supervise construction of the houses. Dudley's endurance as a runner, developed in his youth, came in handy.

"I never worked so hard in my life," Dudley says. "I ran thirty miles a day, six days a week. I had to, in order to get the houses done on time. We were getting them done so fast, I warned farmer Smith's wife she'd better get her cow out of the field we were heading for because we were advancing like the German Blitz." He adds with a laugh, "She said, 'As you advance, my cow will retreat.'"

By now there was no doubt in Dudley's mind that even though he wasn't a mechanical genius like his brother, Harold, he had his own genius for organizing, commanding men and solving problems. The houses in Pictou were his first real experience. At FMF, Dudley had learned how to treat employees. He could get them to work without resentment, a skill he obtained from foreman Joe LeFresne, who, ironically, would work for Dudley later on.

"Never tell someone to do something. Always ask," was what Joe taught Dudley. "If there is any doubt in a worker's mind about your judgement," Joe told him, "make sure he airs it immediately. Never let him have a chance to think about it and build up resentment."

The first time Dudley had a chance to put Joe's advice to the test was on the houses in Pictou. One day, the water boy, perhaps thirteen or fourteen years old, came to Dudley's office upset. One of the men, known as a smart aleck, had dumped a bucket of water over the boy's head as a joke. This was no joke to Dudley. It was a waste of time and, ultimately, money. Dudley asked the boy which crew the man worked on, had the office boy write up a cheque for him, went to the house where he was working and fired him.

After walking away, Dudley realized the other six men

working with the dismissed man might take up his side. Supervising the men constructing these houses carried a tremendous responsibility and Dudley had to show them who was boss. No time could be wasted on a tug of war between management and employees. Time was money. News of a firing would spread quickly and Dudley had to make sure that nothing negative would be said about his part in the matter.

Even though he was alone, Dudley lost no time returning to the house in case someone might question his judgment. Nearly six feet tall, slim and athletic, with dark hair, eyes, and complexion, Dudley still knew he would be no match for six men if they decided to gang up on him. But he also knew he wouldn't be a leader if he showed fear. As he approached the house again, one of the workers, an ex-Mountie, jumped down from the scaffolding in front of Dudley and shouted, "Did you just fire that man?" Dudley was ready for him. "If you have anything to say about me firing that man," he said, his eyes piercing those of the other man, "you say it right now." It was a matter of tone and wills and Dudley knew it. The man went back to work and no more was said about the incident.

Eastern had started out with the converted henhouse, a small attached house used for an office and a small outbuilding for storage. By 1941, Harold and Jim were making enough money to finance their own dry kiln. Harold was a perfectionist when it came to his millwork and felt he could produce higher quality work if the boards he had to work with were properly dried. The best way to ensure that was to build his own kiln.

"Most of the problem," Harold has said, "was that during the war there was a three-year delivery period for most machinery. Well, we couldn't wait that long so I had to build a lot of the things myself. One of the first things I built was a big exhaust fan to take all the shavings out of the plant."

Until 1943, Harold and Jim's company was busy with a heavy load of orders. At the peak of this period, there were, incredibly, 785 men on the company payroll. But the big boom in housing was over for the time being, so the company turned its attention to building sectional MINCA cargo barges, designed by naval architect, William J. Roué, who designed the original *Bluenose*.

The first contract for seventy-five barges was secured from the British Ministry of War. Brookfield's also secured a contract for barges and Harold heard that Brookfield's was setting up their barge production by building a huge wheel which turned the barge for the men working on it. Harold knew a more efficient means of production would

British Ministry of War sectional barge, with Harold G. Mingo (second man just left of the flag, in a hat) leaning on the rail, circa 1944. Eastern mass-produced 162 vessels designed by naval architect, W.J. Roué, Bluenose designer.

be needed if Eastern were to acquire more contracts. This was a highly competitive business.

For the British Ministry of War it was a competition for lives. Equipment had to be produced fast enough to support the Allies. The ministry wanted to award contracts to the company with the most efficient barge production so Harold set out to design an assembly line based on timing: no part of a barge need take more than fifteen minutes to assemble. With the record Dudley had already been setting in housing construction, Harold knew that together — using his design and Dudley's ability to command men — they could do this job in record time too.

Alfred Arbuckle was plant manager, but Dudley would be in charge of the assembly line to build the barges. Brookfield's had 515 men working on the barges, Eastern had 350, yet Eastern was able to produce barges faster, building one barge a day. Winning a contract to do 100 more, Eastern completed all but thirteen of them by the end of the war in 1945. Again, C.D. Howe had played a role in helping Eastern expand its plant in order to build the barges.

Partnerships Change
1945-1951

*B*y 1945, the partnership between Harold and Jim was becoming strained. Because Eastern Woodworkers was doing well, Jim wanted to own the company himself. He took care of the books and was able to make decisions without consulting Harold, much to Harold's chagrin.

"One day I was playing cards with Graham Towsend's wife, who was our bookkeeper, " Harold has said. "'See you bought a new truck,' she said, 'and paid for it with an Eastern cheque even though it has Tidewater Construction written on it.' I didn't know anything about it until then," Harold said.

In total conflict with their agreement, Jim had started his own companies. One, called Tidewater Construction, bought machinery that was being used to load the barges Eastern had constructed. Jim also owned another company called Sydney R. MacKay Lumbering Co. which was selling lumber to Eastern Woodworkers. Eastern was literally feeding Jim's companies.

Harold was not at all happy about the situation but he didn't know what to do because Jim wielded so much power in town. Jim knew he was breaking their partnership agreement, so he tried to get Harold to convert Eastern to a limited company which would allow him to own whatever companies he wanted in addition to Eastern. Harold would only agree to convert Eastern from a partnership to a limited company if he were made a 51% shareholder and Jim would not agree to that. So one day Jim came to Harold and offered to buy him out of Eastern Woodworkers altogether for $50,000.

That kind of money in 1945 was considered a fortune and Harold was tempted. But the document Jim had drawn up stipulated that Harold could not work in the woodworking business for ten years after the partnership was dissolved. Jim certainly understood Harold's role in making Eastern successful and feared competition from any company Harold might start.

"Jim might as well have asked me to bury myself for ten years," Harold has said. "My life was machines, woodworking and tinkering. What would I have done for ten years if I couldn't work in the woodworking business?"

The fact that Jim approached Harold to dissolve their partnership put more stress on their relationship. There wasn't any sense in working with someone who was trying to buy him out, Harold thought. He had to find a way to get out of the partnership with Jim and still be able to continue in the woodworking business. Harold was fighting for his life and his livelihood.

New Glasgow was a very close-knit town and Jim was well known. Harold wasn't sure he could trust a lawyer or an accountant there. He needed Ernie's education and skills to help him because as Harold said, "Ernie had more gall than I." But to get Ernie back from where he was at the time was a problem.

By the time Ernie was twenty-five in 1942, he had

enlisted in the army as an ordinary rank and was soon promoted to lieutenant. While overseas, Ernie was made a commander of a tank unit. When Harold needed help in the fall of 1945, Ernie was still in the army and overseas. If Harold wanted to get Ernie back home he needed advice, so he called his cousin, Edgar Mingo, who was a colonel in the army. Colonel Mingo told Harold that Ernie's employer, before he had enlisted, could apply under Industrial Release. Harold convinced the company to apply and it worked: Ernie was now free to return home.

But as strange as it may seem, Ernie received Harold's telegram with mixed feelings. The war was over and Ernie had become the officers' accountant and sports director, organizing the messes and entertainment with the promise of an educational tour of Europe — all expenses paid — an opportunity he would not likely ever have again. Ernie's loyalty to his brother and Harold's offer of 40% of the shares in the business, however, convinced Ernie to give up the army, board the *Île de France* and return home.

When the ship landed at the dock in Halifax in October of 1945, Harold and Dudley were there to meet Ernie. With 10,000 troops aboard, it took a while for them to find him.

"They were coming off the ship like flies," Dudley says. "Then we realized the officers were coming off from a separate gangplank so we finally saw him."

"The company Harold had applied through to get me home was rather annoyed with me," Ernie says, "because they expected me to come back to work for them. Instead, I went to work for Harold. We went back to New Glasgow and spent all of our time trying to figure out what we were going to do about Jim. I stayed at Harold's.

"One day, when we were at the office, Jim arrived with his accountant from Saint John, New Brunswick. They took the books out of the safe to work on them. We suspected they might be doctoring the books, so when they put the books back in the safe later that day, I called my friend, Jack Lawlor, at the bank, and asked him to come over and change the combination of the safe so that no one could get their hands on the books until we could get them audited. Jack came over, changed the combination and locked the books in the safe.

"Then we didn't know what to do," Ernie continues, "so we called Irvin Barrow of Barrow and Nicoll in Halifax. Irvin told us to call the income tax department and they'd come to get the books to audit them.

"If we hadn't changed the combination of the safe that day," Ernie says with a trace of the excitement he might have felt back then, "they would have taken the books and we wouldn't have been able to do anything about it. It was that close.

"So then it was really bad for Jim," he goes on. "The income tax department came, took the books and Jim had to deal with them. They found out he'd been doing all sorts of things that were illegal. But instead of going to jail, partly because of his father-in-law, Jim was only fined. We settled out of court. Our lawyer told Jim if he gave the plant, lumber, equipment and inventory to Harold, he could walk away from it. Which he did. We didn't have any working capital but within two years, Harold did get $50,000 back from Excess Profit Tax which Eastern had paid into.

"At the time we were negotiating all this," Ernie reveals, "Harold offered me 40% of the business free. Even though I'd made sure Harold had something in writing with Jim, I trusted Harold. He was my brother. We didn't put anything in writing. On April 15, 1946, we opened the doors of Eastern Woodworkers as a partnership — Harold and I. Because we didn't have any working capital, I had to put $3,000 of my own money into it. I hadn't expected to pay anything for my shares after coming all the way back from Europe, but that was the way it was."

With the end of the war and the burden of investigating ownership, work virtually came to a halt at Eastern for six months. The plant had been tooled for war production and no wholesale or retail stores existed yet. Harold and Ernie took this time to reorganize and reequip the plant for peacetime work. They were determined to keep Eastern from becoming a statistic so set about to develop a company that would survive beyond the era of plentiful contracts which the war years had provided. A second dry kiln, much larger than the first, was begun and the stockroom was expanded to provide office space and a retail department for building supplies.

The New Glasgow *Evening News* published an article on April 20, 1946, about the new ownership and reorganizations, stating that the two brothers had expressed "the ambition to get Eastern Woodworkers firmly established as a 'small industry' in the town."

At the same time Harold and Ernie had formed their partnership in Eastern Woodworkers, Dudley, Bill MacLean and Ernie had put up $1,000 each to form a company called Gomac Construction — Go for Mingo and mac for MacLean. Harold put in $1,000, too, as well as some equipment and office space, to become a silent partner without signing authority. Because they were afraid Bill might be overwhelmed by the Mingos, Dudley, Ernie and Harold agreed to give Bill 40% of Gomac and make him president. Dudley would be vice-president and Ernie secretary-treasurer. With 20% each for Dudley, Ernie, and Harold, the Mingos still had 60% of the shares.

Now, at last, by 1946, the three brothers were in business together. Eastern would bid jobs and prefab houses and Gomac would subcontract to erect the houses on site. It wasn't always smooth running, but these men were equally ambitious and willing to take enormous chances to make their businesses work. None of them wanted to end up back on a farm or ever again be in the position of having to depend on others for jobs as he had had to do during the Depression. For Dudley, contracting was his life's work, just as designing and building machines was Harold's. Gomac represented an opportunity for him to run his own company successfully, too.

In 1947, a contract was going to tender for fifty houses in Woodstock, New Brunswick, through Wartime Housing. Even though Eastern and Gomac were located 360 miles away from the site, the companies decided to bid on the job.

"We owed some money to the bank — about $10,000," Ernie discloses. "But we had some accounts owing us so Harold collected these and brought the money to the bank. Instead of allowing us to use the money to bid on the job for Woodstock, the bank manager took the money to put against our debt. Now we didn't have a deposit to put on our bid. I was in Montréal [Québec] at the time to place our bid with Wartime Housing when Harold called to tell me I might as well come back home because we didn't have the money to place the bid.

"Well, there was an engineer at Wartime Housing who was an older gentleman," Ernie continues. "I told him our story and he took pity on us. He told me to put the bid in anyway. That was unheard of then or now but we put our bid in, were low tender and we were on our way. If that engineer hadn't given us a break, we couldn't have gotten started. After that we got Chatham [New Brunswick] and other jobs but it was just little things like the engineer giving us a break that made the difference."

And it was just little things like Ernie's tenacity in speaking to the engineer in the first place that had also made the difference too, allowing Eastern to bid without a deposit, helping to keep the company going. As surely as he knew how to pole jump on the field as a youth, Ernie knew how to get over obstacles in business, too. And he knew how to use his influence with others to get results. After all, he had been a commander in the army.

The Mingos were all perfectly aware of the hierarchy involved in business. Going directly to the top to resolve problems was not intimidating to them. On the contrary, they had learned from their mother that the best results come from influencing those at the top. And that's what they did nine times out of ten: went straight to the top. After all, they wanted to be at the top themselves. They knew the best way to influence those they needed most was to act as men who were on their way. Showing their courage, their confidence and their respect for authority was a practical way of getting where they wanted to go. Ernie, of course, was most equipped to do this because of his training and education. Already in the process of receiving his Registered Chartered and Industrial Account- ant Certificate, Ernie had just that much more "gall," as Harold had said, than either he or Dudley.

When Ernie got back to New Glasgow from Montréal, he was so angry at the bank manager who had refused the loan that he called Irvin Barrow in Halifax and told him he wanted to see the top man at the Royal Bank in Halifax. "Irvin arranged a meeting with him," Ernie says, "and we were guaranteed that Clarey Earl, who was just out of the air force, would look after our accounts in New Glasgow from then on instead of the manager who was there at the time."

So the fifty houses went through after all. Dudley stayed in New Glasgow to supervise prefabricating the houses for Woodstock, while Bill MacLean went to the site to erect the houses with Ernie Sutherland, Don Gould, Eldrige Cameron and Frank McDougall.

"I always joke," Dudley laughs, "that we were so poor

when we prefabbed the houses in New Glasgow and they were ready to be shipped to Woodstock, that we had to tie the big load of houses together with binding tape because we didn't have any money to buy rope. Pretty near, anyway."

Gomac, however, made $15,000 profit on the project which was a fair chunk of change back in those days. Gomac was on its way.

Eastern Woodworkers was another story, however. The years 1946 and 1947 were not good years for Eastern. Everyone seemed to be sighing with relief now the war was over. No one was in any hurry to place orders for cabinetwork or millwork.

To make matters worse Harold had become sick. Medicine had improved considerably since his mother's death but Harold became extremely ill with the same disease his mother had — hyperactive thyroid. For nearly a year, Harold was unable to work. "He was so thin," Dudley says, "he was nothing but skin and bones when I drove him to the train station so he could go to the Lahey Clinic in Boston, Massachusetts, to have his thyroid removed. He shook the whole way there. His nerves were shot."

"The first time I saw Harold after he went to the clinic," Ernie says, "was months later. Marge went to Boston to pick him up and drive him to Montréal to meet me. When I first went into Marge and Harold's hotel room in Montréal, I thought Marge was with a stranger. Harold had gained forty pounds since his thyroid had been removed and I almost didn't recognize him."

Until he became sick, Harold had been a workaholic. For seventeen years and more, Harold, like his mother, nearly worked himself into the ground. But after his recovery, Harold never worked as hard again. The condition knocked the workaholic out of him. Besides, now he had his younger brothers and Bill with him. He could trust them and they were tremendously capable men themselves. Being in business with them meant some pressures were taken off Harold.

The year Harold was sick, Ernie ran Eastern himself. It was a struggle but there was another thing in Eastern's favour: most of the old established companies had gone out of business; either the owners had died, lost interest or gone bankrupt. Brookfield's was still around but was Eastern's only real competitor.

In 1948, there was quite a stir generated when a sales representative for Tip Top Tailors came to Eastern to see the prefabs. He went back to Toronto, Ontario, and told the owners of the chain about Eastern's prefab buildings. The owners invited Harold and Ernie to fly to Toronto to discuss possibilities for Israel. Apparently, the commanding general of the Israeli army was a Tip Top owner's brother. Tip Top ordered five prefab houses from Eastern, two to go to Ontario as cottages, three to go to Israel.

Ernie Sutherland, one of Eastern's top superintendents, flew to Israel to assemble the houses. Unfortunately, the climate in Israel did not suit wooden buildings. The desert was too hot and there were too many wood-eating insects. Stucco and concrete were more appropriate materials to use in the scorching environment of this new country. No more orders were requested but at least Eastern had had its first taste of international trade.

By 1948, Gomac had so much business it could not get enough lumber to meet its needs. Gomac, unlike Eastern, did not have to depend on the restrictions of prefabricating buildings or specific millwork to survive. Gomac could construct any type or size of building on site. So Eastern built its own sawmill to supply Gomac's contracts and Eastern's orders for prefabs, and either bought logs from local farmers or purchased woodlots to supply the mill.

Again, Harold's ingenuity played a hand in the success of the sawmill. In the early 1940s, Harold had bought a 300 horse power (h.p.) boiler and second-hand Robb engine. With them he designed his own trestles and generator for the manufacturing plant.

By 1948, Harold had to revamp his boiler system for two reasons: the Pictou County Power Board could not supply enough power to meet the needs of the plant and he needed to get rid of the enormous waste of shavings and sawdust accumulated from his expanding wood industry. It was becoming a fire hazard and to remove it would have cost $3-$4,000. To deal with the waste and provide the power, Harold designed a system consisting of

The Brother Street 300 h.p. boiler tower at Eastern's manufacturing plant and sawmill complex. Harold G. Mingo designed and erected the boiler system in the early 1940s.

53

a waste wood-fueled boiler which supplied a steam engine driving an electric generator. Even the Pictou County Power Board could not supply electricity with as much consistency as could Eastern's electrical generating system. Harold had designed and built a recycling system for which anyone in these ecologically conscious times could derive inspiration.

Between 1947 and 1949, Eastern and Gomac completed 189 houses. At one point, in 1947, Eastern and Gomac bid on two jobs: one to move 100 houses from Pictou to New Glasgow and Stellarton, Nova Scotia, and another for 139 houses to be built in New Glasgow, Amherst, Stellarton, and Charlottetown, P.E.I. Ernie priced the materials while Bill and Dudley estimated the labour on the jobs. The tender for the two jobs was due on the same day. Eastern and Gomac were low tenders on both jobs.

"I didn't think we were strong enough financially to handle both jobs," Ernie says. "There were only two bids in: ours and Bob [R.B.] Cameron's [a well-known industrialist today] for Cameron Construction. We were low tender on both but since we couldn't do both, Bob ended up getting the job to move the 100 houses from Pictou even though his prices were high. I always figured we put Bob on his way because if we had taken both jobs, Bob wouldn't have gotten the one he did. With the prices he had, he ended up making about $75,000 profit on the job."

"Back then, Bob didn't have any equipment," Dudley adds. "He came to me to ask to borrow our water pump or five bags of cement or whatever. He didn't have much then, doing those 100 houses in Pictou. I'd give him what he needed."

By 1949, Eastern and Gomac had bid on sixty-six houses along Bayers Road in Halifax. They were low tender on the job but by now, it was more than other contractors in the New Glasgow area who were becoming nervous about Eastern's and Gomac's success: Brookfield's, the largest woodworking and contracting company around, was getting jittery, too. Until 1949, Brookfield's had done just about all the houses in the Halifax area and it did not want Eastern and Gomac horning in on its territory. Using all the political connections they had, Brookfield's tried to stop Eastern and Gomac from securing the tender on the sixty-six houses. Brookfield's demanded that the contract go to tender again and again.

"Just bidding jobs is expensive," Dudley explains. "The third time we had to bid on the sixty-six houses, Ernie pulled a coin out of his pocket and said 'Let's toss this thing to see whether we'll bid again or not. If it's heads, we'll bid; tails, we'll forget the job.' Well, the coin came up heads so we bid on the job the third time and, by golly, we got it."

Dudley spent eight months boarding in Halifax from Monday to Saturday to complete the sixty-six houses, while his family (which now included his wife and five daughters) stayed in New Glasgow. When he completed the last of these houses, Dudley travelled back and forth from New Glasgow to Summerside for a year and a half to build 105 houses there.

If ferry lines and services are horrendous today, they were even worse back then. Roads were just being put through and none were paved. With the red mud of the Island and the infrequently scheduled ferry runs, Dudley had many legitimate complaints about this job.

On one trip to Summerside, Dudley got off the ferry in Borden, P.E.I., at ten o'clock at night. There was a big crowd of people leaving the ferry but they were only able to get five miles outside Borden by midnight because of a snow storm.

"Some people from Mt. Allison ended up by a barn lined with trees in a farmer's yard to find shelter," Dudley says. "I had a half ton truck and a quart of rum. There was a driver of a big truck in back of me so I offered him a drink. After a few drinks, the driver figured he could get his big truck turned around to go back to Borden and he did.

"Well, we got to Borden and all the electricity was out. We got hotel rooms but the lights and heat were out. The guy at the hotel had to take us to our rooms by candlelight. We nearly froze to death that night without heat, and the next day, we couldn't even get breakfast because the electricity was still out. "

Dudley rarely had a chance to see his family now. He would come home Saturday night (back than people worked six days a week) usually at midnight — because it took that long to get the ferry and travel — and leave again by mid-afternoon the next day in order to return in time for work Monday morning.

His wife, Bernice, remembers that he usually came home with seven shirts to be washed and ironed before he left the next day. In those days, there were no automatic washers, only wringer washers, and no dryers. The shirts were usually of starched cotton and ironing them was a chore indeed. Little time was left for them to be together. Once Dudley left, Bernice had to take care of the household needs and five children alone. This was as difficult a time for her as it was for him.

And it was for the children too. Around this time Dudley was a complete stranger, and even terrified the youngest, who had rarely seen him in the first years after her birth. Apparently, when he came home from P.E.I., Dudley put his arms out for her to come to him. Instead, she jumped into her sister's arms, frightened of his gruff voice and manner. More than once she hid under the table when Dudley spoke to discipline her. For the most part, the children were used to living with their mother and their giggling sisters. To have this larger-than-life presence occasionally in the house was intimidating. This was a man used to dealing with hundreds of tough men and he would not always know how to turn off that commanding voice when he came home.

And yet, life was much more exciting when Dudley was home. The house seemed to take on a life of its own when he was there. In time, each little daughter eagerly awaited his return. Bernice would make sure the girls were all bathed and in their best clothes, and all six of them, Bernice included, would run to the window frequently, in anticipation of his arrival.

By 1949, the partnership between Harold and Ernie was on shaky ground. Until then, Eastern had not shown a profit. When the financial statements came out in 1949, Ernie realized he had only been given 20% of the profits, not the 40% he expected. Ernie was very upset about his portion of the shares. He had given up a promising career in the army to work with Harold. Now he wasn't receiving the share of the business promised him. "Everyone wanted 10% of the profits but not 10% of the losses, " Harold once remarked.

In frustration and anger, Ernie, by now married to Eve Shepley, took her on a trip to Calgary, Alberta, to scout out opportunities there. Ernie was ready to leave Eastern. When he returned from Calgary, however, Harold pacified him. Harold had plans to incorporate Eastern with Gomac, and when the two companies became incorporated, Ernie would receive more shares. Ernie felt he had to have faith in Harold's plan or he would be giving up a lot. It may have been too late for his career in the army; but Ernie already had more money in Eastern than he did in Gomac and he knew he would lose everything he had worked for if he left. So he decided not to go to Calgary but to stay with Harold instead. In 1950, Ernie, thirty-three, received his Registered Industrial and Chartered Accounts Certificate.

Contracting orders were so numerous in 1950, especially for lumber, that more efficient means of transporting lumber were required to reach all corners of the lot — now eighteen acres of the mill, plant, kilns, offices and store.

"Don't be surprised one of these days if you see a Ford tractor wallowing along on stilts and apparently sitting on a load of lumber," read the first lines of an article written in the *Evening News* commemorating the completion of a "home-brew outfit" Harold invented to meet trans-portation needs. The Straddler, as it became known, was the first straddle carrier in eastern Canada. British Colum-bia and parts of the States had them, but there were none anywhere else in Canada, except Harold's, which is amazing considering the number of straddle carriers one sees today.

The design consisted of a tractor with an extra transmission attached to slow it down to a top speed of thirteen miles an hour and to give it more power. The frame was of plate steel, bent for streamlining by Maritime Steel, and welded at Eastern's metal shop. The wheels, from an old truck, provided independent steering and drew power from overgrown bike-type chains and cogs (or sprockets) which came directly from the tractor. Hydraulics which once operated the landing gear of a four engine Liberator bomber in the war days picked up the load of lumber.

Apparently, the *Evening News* felt it necessary to warn the people of New Glasgow about the new machine "so you won't think your eyes are playing tricks on you when

The Straddler on a New Glasgow Street, circa 1950. Eastern's Harold G. Mingo designed this straddle carrier (used to move and position heavy loads of lumber) which was the first of its kind in eastern Canada.

you see it coming. And also so you can take pride in what can get done in Pictou County."

The bottom floor of an old red brick building at Parkdale in New Glasgow was rented to supply more room for storage, and once again the office building was expanded and renovated, with Peruvian pine, to provide more space for a store and several offices. A retail store was also opened in Antigonish, Nova Scotia.

But by the end of 1950, Gomac had an abundance of work; Eastern Woodworkers did not. Eastern might have been contracting the jobs to prefabricate houses, and subcontracting the assembly of them on the site to Gomac, but Eastern was not making (and had never made) much money on its end. Gomac was, and besides, since Gomac did not have to depend on contracts for prefabricated houses or buildings to survive, its potential for doing business was greater.

Looking at the situation, Barrow and Nicoll, who had become the accountants for Gomac as well as Eastern, could see that Gomac would probably do even better in the future. They were concerned for their first client, Harold, now that his company was not doing as well. But once again Harold's shrewdness paid off. He decided it was time to gain control of Gomac and he figured out how to go about it. Harold's argument was that he had contributed not only $1,000 for shares in Gomac (just as everyone else had) but also equipment to the company. His shares, therefore, should have been worth more. In other words, Harold was saying he actually owned 51% of Gomac or controlling interest.

In the document drawn up, Gomac was absorbed with each of the Gomac partners becoming a shareholder of Eastern Woodworkers Limited. Ernie would receive 22% of the shares because he had invested in both companies, and Bill and Dudley would receive 6% each. Ernie would have to pay Harold $11,000 for his shares, Dudley and Bill $3,000 for each of theirs. Harold would own 66% of the shares and since he had already owned Eastern for over ten years, he didn't have to pay anything for his shares.

Needless to say, there was a great row among the partners about this one.

Ernie was shocked to learn he would be getting only 22% of the shares and would also be expected to pay $11,000 for them. At first Ernie refused to sign the document. But then he realized in the long run, he would still benefit from incorporating the two companies. As it was, he was only getting 20% from Eastern and 20% from

Gomac. Combining the two companies would mean he would receive 2% more shares. It wasn't much, but it was in his own best interest to incorporate.

Bill MacLean felt trapped and definitely unhappy about the situation. For him the choice was death by sledgehammer or noose — neither was palatable. He had always been overpowered by the Mingos. No one had more to lose through incorporation than Bill. He already owned 40% of Gomac, which was doing well. Now he would only have 6% of the "new" limited company and would have to pay more money for his shares in it.

For Dudley, the fight was for independence and control. If woodworking and machinery were Harold's life, contracting and construction were Dudley's. Dudley had already worked five years for FMF, five years for Harold at Eastern Woodworkers and nearly five years with his own company, Gomac Construction. To sign would mean giving away his self-reliance.

A trying time for all, their relationships were strained, including their personal ones. Dudley went to Toronto to think about his situation, to decide whether or not he should set up business somewhere in the Toronto area. But like all of them, Dudley was a product of the Great Depression. He knew a dollar did not come easily. His family had already suffered his long absences and had given up much so he could have his own business. To start over again would be very difficult.

Dudley's business in Nova Scotia was already established and doing very well. His work situation would be virtually the same, even though ownership would change — he would still be able to hire the men he had grown to know and trust and he would still be competing with the same companies.

And yet, there was a big difference between what Dudley and Bill owned in Gomac, a successful company, and what they would own in Eastern Woodworkers, a shaky one. Eastern would now be able to take profits from construction to feed stores and plants which were tenuous at best. So when Dudley came back from Toronto, he refused to sign the documents until the accountants told him, in no uncertain terms, that he had a choice: either sign, or he would be forced to sell his shares in Gomac and be denied shares in Eastern. "With a mortgage and five children," Dudley says, "I felt like I had a gun to my head."

At the signing, Dudley banged his fist on the table and told Harold and his accountants that if Ernie, Bill and he decided to leave them right then and there, they would never find another three to replace them. They could hire men, but they would either be drunk, too lazy, out playing golf or stealing. They would never be able to replace Ernie, Bill and him.

Dudley was right and they all knew it, but Ernie had more to gain by the incorporation than he would lose; Bill felt like a puppet to the brothers; and Harold had the best lawyers and accountants in Halifax to back up his argument — that the equipment he had given them five years earlier was worth more than anyone else's original investment.

One would think that Ernie and Dudley could have made a legal case against Harold, but neither was willing to pit himself against his older brother in court. Unlike Harold who was a loner, Ernie and Dudley felt that sticking together as a family was more important than alienating themselves from one another. The whole ordeal, nonetheless, left bitter tastes in their mouths forever after.

Yet the focus of these men was on the future, not the past. Some resentment would always remain but not to the extent that it would interfere with their goals or their sense of brotherhood, because despite everything, three of these men were brothers, soul mates from a common background and equally ambitious. They worked together and partied together.

Within months, they were almost as they once were: working harder than most could ever bear and blowing off steam at every opportunity. They loved to gather in the evenings, to sing, to dance, to encourage anyone to play musical instruments, to drink rum and to tell stories of their youth, including the pranks they pulled on each other. There was more laughter at this time than any other. These men grasped life and lived it to the fullest. Their spirits were infectious and drew people to them so that their houses were always full, permeated with vitality.

There was no question Harold was the kingpin. A deference towards him saturated the air. Everyone was in awe of him. Harold was shrewd, intelligent and a genius at inventing and the newspapers articles confirmed this. Yet each of the other partners had a sense of pride in themselves, too. Dudley, perhaps as at no other time in his life, felt indispensable and truly trusting in his own talent: why otherwise would his oldest brother try to obtain control of his company? Ernie, quietly aware of his more advanced education, knew they all relied totally on his business acumen. Bill was a confident man too and knew the Mingos would search high and low before they would find another like him. He did not participate in the blowout parties as the Mingos did, preferring to enjoy his off-hours with his own family; but he knew he was an integral part of a company on the road to success and gave his all to ensure its winning direction.

Once Harold took control of Gomac, they were all practical enough to realize they each had to pitch in to make a go of it. At least Bill, Ernie, and Dudley would still be working together, and Bill and Dudley would now have an interest in the woodworking and retailing parts of the business which they had not had before. They knew from past performance that if they could reap their share of the meagre profits from now on, then the amalgamation could solidify their efforts to succeed. After all, Harold was a genius at mechanics and inventing; Dudley a master at organizing, commanding men and solving construction problems; and Ernie was a wizard at finances. With that kind of winning combination, they could not fail.

The formation of the new Eastern Woodworkers Limited took place in 1951. The officers of the company were: Harold G. Mingo, president; Ernest C. Mingo, secretary-treasurer and general manager; Dudley L. Mingo, director and construction superintendent; and J. William MacLean, director and projects manager. From then on, because the partners were becoming more and more aware of their success, and because of the numerous times they met and had to read minutes of the previous meetings, they began, somewhat in jest, to call each other by their respective initials: H.G., E.C., D.L. and J.W.

A Leader in Atlantic Canada
1951-1965

With the onset of the Korean War in 1950, following the aftermath of the recent Second World War, came the scare of a Third World War. The Government of Canada feared the Russians would invade the strategic border in the Arctic between Canada and Russia. Officials decided prefabricated huts would have to be constructed as quickly as possible to ensure adequate housing for armed forces in the event of an attack. The government considered all companies in Canada with experience in building prefabrication as possible producers of the huts, but narrowed it down to two after Northwood Construction Company went bankrupt: Eastern Woodworkers and a company from Western Canada.

Harold had received feedback about the company out west. Apparently the owner of the Manitoba company refused to listen to the inspectors and his workers were doing badly on their 100 huts. Harold did listen and predicted that if Eastern tooled (or "jigged" as they would say) the plant properly for the preliminary contract for seventy-five huts, Eastern would avoid the problems facing the other company. With $125,000 taken from various contracting profits and loans, Eastern jigged for production at the Parkdale site, gambling they would win other contracts over the company out west.

A commander from Ottawa, Ontario, came to Nova Scotia to witness a test for the assembly of the huts. Dudley selected a crack crew and supervised them for the demonstration. Sufficiently impressed, the commander asked how many huts Eastern could produce in a week or a month. "As many as you like," he was told. The partners knew producing the huts efficiently was just a matter of organization and manpower. They were organized and they would find the manpower. They wanted to be given the chance to prove what they could do.

Soon after that, Ottawa put out tenders to build another 2,000 huts. In a bid that included K.C. Irving and Brookfield's, Eastern won a $4.3 million contract for another 500 huts. The company's exceptional record with the first seventy-five huts coupled with a good word from Senator Hawkins who represented Nova Scotia in Ottawa at the time had contributed to their success. Of the five plants across Canada who won contracts to build the huts, Eastern's share was the largest. And Ottawa even hired a private plane to fly the other manufacturers in to New Glasgow to see exactly how Eastern was producing them.

"We agreed to allow these sons-a-guns to come down to show them our secrets," says Ernie unhappily, "and this guy from Edmonton tried to hire our production manager, Art Richardson, right from under our noses. He didn't succeed, but we were quite put out that he'd tried."

Newspapers all over Canada heralded Eastern's

67

accomplishment of acquiring the contract to manufacture the 500 huts. In the New Glasgow *Evening News* of August 14, 1951, an editorial headline boasted: "Something Else to Be Proud About." Part of the editorial referred to the closure of a coal mine which had employed 400 men and how Eastern "will not replace the Allan Shaft entirely; not nearly so. But [the order for 500 huts] is certainly a step in the right direction. "

The editorial was wrong in presuming Eastern would not provide employment for as many people as the Allan Shaft. As a matter of fact, Eastern would eventually employ more people than any other industry in Pictou County. But the editorial was accurate when it went on to say "at first there were those who saw [Eastern] only as a wartime industry. The men at the top of it, however, were not content to go out of business when the war was over. They went on the lookout for new ideas and new markets. That they did so with success is a matter of record." And the editorial also recognized "the brains" that had put the deal together. "Presumably," the article reads, "Harold Mingo's genius for assembly line woodworking was back of it all; but we rather imagine that others in the organization contributed ideas here and there. The sum total of this brainy endeavour, however, was success and the adoption of the technique over the nation."

"You should have walked through the assembly line," Dudley says with pride in his brother's achievement. "It was just like Ford building cars. Harold and Carl MacLanders put together the machinery, and Carl was just like Harold—everything had to be perfect. Anyone else putting the machines together for the assembly line would have used wood and slapped them together in a week. Not Harold. He used steel so nothing would warp. Once Harold put something together, it was there to stay."

"We made a $1 million profit on those huts," Ernie

says. "Harold had the accountants invest most of it in debentures after taxes, but if I were running it I wouldn't have kept that plant once the huts were finished. I would have been building apartment buildings. The plant was Harold's baby, though, and he had controlling share."

"Yeah," says Dudley, "and one night about a year or so later, when we were sitting around Harold's kitchen table drinking rum, I hit the table and said, 'When we made this massive profit, why didn't you slide me $25,000?' Marge said, 'It's too late now.'"

The Canadian Government wanted housing erected throughout the Maritimes to accommodate armed forces personnel needed for any conflicts brought on by the Korean War. Eastern built 100 houses in Chatham, for the Royal Canadian Air Force (RCAF) and 100 more houses in Eastern Passage, Nova Scotia, for the Royal Canadian Navy (RCN) at Shearwater. Dudley personally supervised construction of the houses for Shearwater from September 1951 to September 1952, which meant he had to leave his family in New Glasgow and travel again. Generally, Bill MacLean travelled too, but only for a day or two at a time, which meant he could live in New Glasgow.

When Newfoundland joined Confederation in 1949, all sorts of potential business opened up — if one were willing to take advantage of the opportunities. Eastern was. In 1952, it bid on and secured a contract for 100 houses in St. John's, Newfoundland, and since this was new territory, Dudley felt compelled to move there to make sure the job would be done properly.

In a ten-year period, Dudley had been away from his home and his family in New Glasgow for a total of four years. He knew that sheer distance between St. John's and New Glasgow would prevent commuting on weekends as he had been able to do during other projects. He was afraid of being trapped on an unfamiliar island of rock and fog without his family. So this time Dudley took them with him.

While Dudley and his family were aboard the boat to Newfoundland, a fierce storm struck. With the ship bobbing on the ocean like a cork, the cargo slammed from one side of the hold to the other. Everyone on board was sick including the family cat whose life was in peril; the cat's incessant howling tempted fellow passengers to throw it overboard. Dudley was one of the few passengers who did not get sick during the harrowing voyage. "I couldn't," he says. "I had a wife and five children on board. I was afraid we weren't going to make it to Newfoundland. I sat up all night on the floor smoking cigarettes, worrying."

1952 was a good year for all of them. As project manager, Bill MacLean flew back and forth between Nova Scotia and Gander, Newfoundland, where Eastern had secured a contract to build 100 houses. With the contract for military huts and the numerous contracts for houses and buildings throughout the Atlantic provinces, Eastern was evolving into one of the largest contracting and lumber companies in eastern Canada. Their credit rating was almost unlimited. And from then on, because of the incorporation of the contracting company, Eastern was able to provide its own financing.

By this time, the Mingos' youngest brother, Carl, had come to work with them. Carl had probably disliked the farm more than anyone in the family. When Dudley was running the farm, he had to take Carl by the collar, march him down around the pumphouse and shove him towards the field to get him to go get the cows. After Harold, Dudley and Ernie had left the farm, Allison had to hire Stan Harrington to do the work. Carl refused to do it.

In 1940, when Carl was seventeen, he had already worked for FMF. The job, which he obtained through

Dudley, had made it possible for him to leave the farm. After he arrived in New Glasgow, Carl lived with Dudley and his family for a few months until he could get his own room at a boarding house. Then he had worked for Harold until 1943, when the army had drafted him.

At the time he was supposed to go for training at Camp Borden in Ontario, and then be sent overseas. Carl, very tall at 6'2" and very handsome, was also extremely thin. He had never been as rough and tumble as Dudley and Ernie, and now he was feeling very weary. Unfortunately, his sergeant thought he was just trying to get out of work.

Ernie had gone through officer training with the sergeant's officer, and when the officer came to Ernie to ask him about Carl before putting him up on charges, Ernie came to his brother's defense. Carl might have tried to get out of the farm work, but he wasn't lazy. Ernie told the officer that Carl must have something physically wrong with him and insisted that Carl be sent to the hospital for tests before any charges were pressed. Carl was admitted to hospital and diagnosed with tuberculosis.

For over two years, Carl remained in a sanatorium in Kentville, Nova Scotia. No one expected him to live. At one point, Harold and Dudley took Allison to see Carl.

When Allison then became sick himself, Harold and Dudley obtained permission to take Carl out of the sanatorium to see his father for one last time. Allison had become very thin himself; his skin had turned yellow. No one knew what was wrong with him. A week after Harold and Dudley had taken Carl to see their father on the farm in 1944, Allison died at sixty-one. Dudley was made executor of the will and the farm was sold to its present owner.

"I didn't know, " Ernie says sadly, "when I said good-bye to Father before I went overseas that that would be the last time I'd see him."

By 1947, Carl was able to leave the sanatorium to attend Pictou Academy, where he finished high school. From there he went to Mount Allison University in Sackville, New Brunswick, for two years, and then to Dalhousie University in Halifax, for two more years to complete his Bachelor of Commerce degree.

When he finished university in 1951, Carl became the fourth Mingo brother to join Eastern. Even though Brother Street in New Glasgow had not been named for the Mingo brothers, it certainly had been an appropriate street for Harold to have set up his first business. Carl began in the office and was soon appointed office manager and later, purchasing manager to look after the huge orders Eastern required.

Because the army huts had been a booming success for Eastern, Harold felt there was unlimited potential in the industry for prefabricated buildings generally. He had heard that the pulp and paper industry wanted a design of a portable building for men working in the woods to use.

Doug Sproull, a young engineer from New Glasgow, was working on the the pulp and paper industry design at the time and Harold approached him with a good offer from Eastern — which he accepted. With the Canadian army's permission, Harold and Doug created an efficient design based on the prefabricated huts Eastern had produced for the army. Eastern was now on its way to producing and selling not only camps for various industries, but also prefab houses of its own design.

To commemorate Eastern's new role in the

72

73

construction industry, the *Canadian Woodworker,* an industry magazine, dedicated an extensive article to the New Glasgow firm. Eastern "constitutes one of the largest and most successful woodworking enterprises in the Maritimes," the article read. "The number of persons on the payroll varies anywhere from 300 to 700, depending on the jobs in hand, and from eight to ten million board feet of lumber is used annually in the firm's production of prefabricated buildings, sash, door, cabinets, store fixtures, mouldings, hardwood flooring and general millwork."

The article offered a detailed description of Eastern's new "MacGregor" houses. The first order for thirty-one prefabs went to British Overseas Airways Corporation (BOAC) in 1952 to house airline personnel stationed at

MacGregor House components destined for Goose Bay, Labrador, circa late 1950s. Eastern designed and began producing these prefabricated wooden houses in the early 1950s, seen here aboard a Maritime Central Airways Bristol aircraft.

Gander. The houses were 40'x 24' with three bedrooms, a dining room, living room, kitchen and bathroom. Constructed of 159 wall and roof panels, mostly 4'x8', the wall panels were 2"x3" spruce and covered with 5/16" plywood outside and 1/4" plywood inside. Several pictures of Harold's production lines and equipment were also presented in the article. One was of the three h.p. horizontal drill press Harold had designed with a separate end spindle powered by a half h.p. motor. Another was a machine made from two Dewalt radial saws. With a pneumatic control system, the machine made a fast, accurate double-end cut-off saw for short members required in door and window frame production. Jigged to produce forty prefab houses a month, Eastern also produced one of the few two-floor prefabs in wood available anywhere at the time.

From September 1953 to September 1955, after Dudley had moved back to New Glasgow from St. John's, he again commuted to Halifax from New Glasgow to complete Spryfield High School and a contract with the Canadian army for 180-man barracks.

Eastern had already been doing work in Gander since 1952 supervised by Frank McDougall. Bill MacLean flew over frequently as project manager. But when Dudley had barely finished the barracks and the high school, Eastern took on numerous other projects in Gander which required him to pack his bags and take his family so he could remain full-time as project manager. He thought he would never have to leave Nova Scotia again, but the jobs in Gander were a massive responsibility. He could not trust them to anyone else if they were to break even, let alone make a profit. The job, literally, was to build the town.

When he arrived in Gander with his family in September, 1955, Dudley discovered that even though Eastern had already built some buildings, there was still very little to the town — only one store, Totman's, in the New Townsite. Schools, churches and other stores were set up in the old army barracks in what was called the Old Townsite left behind by the American army after the war.

This time, Dudley left his furniture back in New Glasgow. An Eastern-designed-and-built MacGregor house was being set up for him, but Dudley had to buy every bit of furniture new for his house. So he went to the few stores there were in the Old Townsite and breezed through saying, "I'll take one of these and one of those. Two of these, four of those." The store owners scurried behind Dudley with pen and paper in hands, jotting down lists of items he wanted delivered when his house was finished. It was quite a sight.

Until the house in the New Townsite was ready, Dudley and his family lived in the Gander Hotel at the old airport. They had to keep their ears covered to muffle the painful roar of the airplane engines as they took off and landed no more than a few feet away from their windows.

Being solely responsible for the construction of a whole new town in the middle of the wilderness of Canada's youngest, and in many ways harshest province was not an easy job. When Dudley first came to Gander, a superintendent had already been overseeing the construction of the various projects for Eastern. Dudley arrived at work at seven o'clock in the morning, the super at nine or ten o'clock.

"How the hell can you make any money getting to work at that hour in the morning?" Dudley wanted to

---

OPPOSITE:
Gander Amalgamated School, Gander, Newfoundland, prior to official opening, November 1, 1957. Eastern served as the contractors for this 500-foot long community school containing "an acre of floor tile." Atlantic Films, St. John's, Newfoundland

know. The super said he spent a lot of time on the job at night. "I don't, " Dudley roared, "I don't have to." Often spending twelve hours and more a day on the job, Dudley always worked during the most efficient part of the day — when all other businesses were operating — and that was not at night.

Within two months, Dudley had to fire the super-intendent, not just because of the hours he kept, but because the super had fired people over foolish things, more as a show of his authority than anything else. Dudley felt authority was earned by fairness and strength, not by how many men one could brag about having fired. Often having to fire men himself, Dudley usually did so out of principle, a fact which helped develop respect from the men who remained. They knew Dudley would give them a second chance if they deserved one.

One super in Grand Falls, Newfoundland, for instance, was drinking on the job. "Dan, you're drinking," Dudley said.

"Yes, " the super said feebly.

"The next time I get a call saying you're drinking, I'm going to fire you," Dudley warned.

Inevitably, Dudley received another call about the super's drinking. He jumped in his car and drove from Gander to Grand Falls to make sure for himself. Sure enough, the super had been drinking, so Dudley fired him. All Dan could say was, "Yeah, okay," because he had already been warned.

Another time when Dudley's foreman, Lawrence King, a good man and conscientious worker tried to fire a man much larger than himself, the man beat Lawrence up. Dudley was in his office when Lawrence came in all bloodied. Not willing to tolerate any meanness in a person, Dudley, enraged, went directly to the bunkhouse where the accused man boarded and size or no size, ordered the

Gander Newfoundland, circa 1956. Eastern built eighty percent of the new town between 1952 and 1960. The Gander Amalgamated School is in the dark patch at the centre of the photo.

Department of Transport

man out. Grabbing his belongings on his way, the man flew out the door.

There is no doubt that a major reason Dudley always made profits on his projects was because of the rapport he had with his men. He treated them fairly, inspired them to do their work well and in turn, they worked effectively towards making profits for the company. If Dudley could not find decent men to work for him, he would not have anyone work for him at all. When he found out some of his men were torturing a cat and killing its kittens as a source of amusement, in revulsion Dudley fired the lot of them. He had a tough job to do but he was not going to compromise his sense of justice to do it.

In the three years Dudley worked in Gander, he built eighty percent of the New Townsite — schools, churches, stores, houses, transmitter station and the like. Despite the fact he had been reluctant to go to Gander in the first place, and was quite happy to leave, Dudley's stay in Gander was one of the happiest in his life.

The town had grown from a few hundred people when Dudley first arrived, to several thousand by the time he left. He knew most of them. It was a time of development and excitement. People came to Gander from all over the world to set up businesses. The first to arrive were representatives of the airlines and later merchants, teachers and entrepreneurs. Famous people often stopped over in Gander on their way overseas. Since Gander had only one bar, The Big Dipper at the airport, Gander residents had the opportunity to learn much from the numerous travellers who whiled away their time with refreshments from the bar before departures to all parts of the world.

Along with all the good times and success in business, however, there are always the bad times and failures. At one moment a company's position may seem very secure, the next, it might seem best to pack it all in. Such was the case with Eastern.

In 1955, Eastern had acquired the contract for 215 houses to be constructed at Gagetown, New Brunswick. A fair order to fill, the owners of Eastern were ecstatic with the prospects but soon realized the job in Gagetown was nothing but trouble. The superintendent on the job was a good man but he was not Dudley or Bill and they couldn't be everywhere.

For starters, the houses were an army project, so some materials had to be purchased from one particular company which was forever sending short orders because it did not have enough to keep everyone supplied. The caliber of labour was poor and all labour and carpenters had to be hired through the union. Then the roads were not put in. Diamond Construction was supposed to put them through but took months getting around to it. Eastern was held up getting stuck in the mud paths they had beaten out. Perhaps unwisely, Eastern decided to put the roads through themselves. They thought it was the only way to salvage something from the contract. Then the heating contractor went bankrupt. And the sheet rock was put on damp lumber so nails popped out all over the place when it dried.

Eastern lost $250,000 on the project. They were not alone in their misery, however. Brookfield's, the largest construction firm at the time, went bankrupt over jobs in Gagetown which they could not fulfil.

Eastern bounced back quickly, however. Dudley made $350,000 profit from the work in Gander over a period of less than two years alone. He made $190,000 on ninety-six houses in one year, $100,000 on the school and during the three years from 1955 to 1958 that he was in Gander, Dudley totalled profits of over $500,000. He sent a cheque for $350,000 to New Glasgow to cover the losses on the job in Gagetown. Dudley not only saved Eastern, but also, along with his partners, could boast of owning and operating the largest construction company in the Atlantic provinces because by then, in 1957, Brookfield's no longer existed.

"Do you know," says Dudley still feeling angry, "I saved Eastern by working and slaving . . . to make a massive profit and the office sent me over a bonus from New Glasgow of $2,000. Out of the $500,000 profit I made they sent me a measly $2,000. I was highly insulted. My shares weren't worth the powder to blow them to hell."

Making profits and being successful is no easy feat. Achievement did not come without struggle for all of them. Once, for instance, in the winter of 1954, Ernie and Bill had worked all night preparing a tender, leaving the office after seven-thirty in the morning. They were exhausted, and had just reached their homes when a call came through informing them that part of the roof of the airport hangar at Shearwater, which Eastern had built, had collapsed, blowing the buses, cars and men right out of the building. No one was seriously hurt, but tired or not, Ernie and Bill had to drive immediately to Halifax in the middle of winter to deal with the situation.

Bill and Ernie drove in Ernie's car; Harold and his son, Floyd, drove in Harold's. When they arrived in Halifax, they contacted their lawyer and then went to inspect the building. That night, sleep deprived, they tried to drive back to New Glasgow in a bitterly cold snowstorm. Harold and Floyd managed to get through, but Bill and Ernie's car became stuck in snow at Lyon's Brook. Ernie knew some people in the village so he and Bill rapped on their door, even though it was well after midnight, and stayed the night there.

In the House of Commons in Ottawa, C.D. Howe said that Eastern was a prominent construction company and would rebuild the roof of the hangar, but the legal ramifications of the collapsed roof took until 1960 to settle, when the court ruled that Eastern would be reimbursed $300,000.

Yet another time, in 1955, Eastern was tied up with a piddling project to move a church hall in Gander. Before turning the reins over to Dudley in Gander, Bill MacLean and Frank McDougall had made an agreement with the Anglican church to move the hall. "I was so busy with this massive project to build Gander," Dudley says, "I forgot about this building for the church. I was desperately busy without that silly old building out there.

"One day, church people came to me and said: 'Mingo, you better get that building out of there, the windows are being broken.' I sent men out to cover every window with plywood. Then they came again and said: 'Move it.' I said:

'I'm not in the moving business. I'm trying to build a town here.' Well, I had to move it because it was Eastern's responsibility.

"Bill came over from New Glasgow and he got two tractors and big timber under it. By this time it was the fall of the year, frost is in the ground and there's a heavy snow. And this job was only peanuts! Bill moved one section. Well, you talk about the lugging and slaving and beating and pounding and the traffic. He gets it to the foundation, leaves it there and with the frost it all goes raggedy and half torn to hell.

"So now I get railroad ties; I'm not going to move the other half the same way. I get the thing down there and the church people call me into the lion's den. They said: 'You broke some of the joists on the first section.' So I put in new joists. Then they call me into the lion's den again and told me I didn't do enough work on the building. I told them: 'I'm not doing another thing on it. I'm all through!'

"Well they tried to sue us for $80,000. Ernie, and Alec MacIntosh, our lawyer, had to go to St. John's for two weeks for the court case. We had to hire another lawyer there because Alec couldn't practice in Newfoundland. So this little job became a monster."

"Fortunately," Ernie says, "Bill took pictures of the move. The building in the pictures was as straight as a die and the windows were all closed up. The pictures destroyed their argument. We did our job. Once we set the building by the foundation that was it for us. When frost came out of the ground, the building went every which way but that wasn't our fault. The court costs for us, though, were something else — $10,000 in 1956!"

"Just as an aside," Ernie continues with a laugh, "I brought a bottle of rum with me in my briefcase to the hotel and when I was setting the briefcase down, the bottle broke. All the documents for the court case were in my briefcase so they got soaked with rum. We had to lay all the papers out and dry them. We ended up presenting these crumpled, rum-soaked documents in court the next day."

With all the commuting required to meet the needs of contracts located in every Atlantic province and beyond, some Eastern employees had a large store of travel adventures to share. For example, in Grand Falls, Eastern had worked on a school and one time Ernie and Laird Fairn (an architect on many of Eastern's Newfoundland projects) had a meeting with the trustees of the school. The session lasted well past midnight and long after the last ferry at Bishop Falls, Newfoundland, had left. Dudley called the man who ran the ferry and offered him money to make the crossing again, which he agreed to do. They arrived back in Gander only to be fogged in. The Gander airport was shut down for nearly a week which meant Ernie and Laird could not get back to Nova Scotia.

"We heard a Scandinavian plane was coming through so we took it," Ernie says. "We went to New York, then took Trans-Canada to Montréal and from there went to Halifax. Well, when we got to Halifax, the airport was closed because of snow so we went to Greenwood [Nova Scotia] and circled around there. The pilot said he'd try one more time to land in Greenwood and if he couldn't, he'd go to Harman Field, Newfoundland. We couldn't believe it! After all that time and distance travelling, we'd be heading back to Newfoundland! Fortunately," Ernie chuckles, "we were able to land in Greenwood so we could take a bus from there to New Glasgow."

There are many personal stories connected with this highly productive period in Eastern's history. One of Harold's came as a result of a major contract Eastern had to construct a mining complex for Canadian British Aluminum in the Baie Comeau area of Québec. During a visit to the project, Harold spotted a boy about sixteen

Canadian British Aluminum Co. mining complex, Baie Comeau, Québec, circa 1955.

years old in town one day. The teenager had been bicycling and had stopped to talk to a couple of people he knew. He spoke to one in French, to the other in English. Harold asked the boy if he would work for him as his interpreter. The boy agreed. His name was Brian Mulroney.

Eastern's good reputation was gradually spreading. In addition to the imposing projects Dudley was supervising in Gander, Bill was project manager for 107 houses for the Department of National Defence (DND) in Saint Margaret's, New Brunswick; for 133 houses in Camp Gagetown; for the physics and engineering building at Mount Allison University in Sackville and for a nineteen-classroom school in Camp Gagetown. Anyone connected with the construction industry in Canada knew Eastern.

By now nearly 1000 people worked for them and the sweetness of success was beginning to show for the partners. They had good times — great feasts of lobsters and steaks, hunting trips, journeys to unfamiliar and sometimes exciting places. There were great opportunities for them to meet new and well-known people.

Harold built a beautiful stucco house during the war in New Glasgow on the East River Road. It had five bedrooms, a circular staircase, a den with a brick fireplace and Peruvian pine walls, rec room, dining room with built-in cabinets and a huge double garage with a guest loft above it. His house was (and still is) called "the gingerbread house on East River Road" because it has a fairy-tale aura about it. In 1945, he also built a large three-bedroom log house overlooking Chance Harbour, Nova Scotia, which also had a small guest house. His wife, Marge, had an abundance of fur coats, diamond rings, paintings, antiques and knickknacks.

Ernie built a modern stucco house in a good area of New Glasgow in 1949, a cottage at Pictou Landing in 1946 and a two-unit apartment building for investment. Bill bought a house very much like Harold's but not as well known because it was located on Albert Street.

Dudley retained his Dutch Colonial house on Albert Street no matter where he happened to live. Not in the best area of town, Dudley's house was next to the lumber yard at Eastern. He had been lucky to get the house during the war, as a moratorium had been placed on new house construction to keep reserves intact for the war effort. It was only because Eastern was completing three of the last houses to be sold before the moratorium that Dudley had

---

been able to get the house but he had had no choice about where it would be located.

Dudley always kept drawings of the house he wanted to build; but he never had the chance to build it, or have a cottage of his own (except for a brief time in Gander) until 1969, because he moved so often. Most of the houses Dudley lived in were scouted out by someone at Eastern before he arrived in a town or city with his family and these rarely suited his personal tastes.

But food was on their tables, and they could buy all the latest gadgets — fridges, hi-fi equipment, televisions, movie cameras, dishwashers, automatic washers and dryers. Harold always drove Lincoln Continentals, and it was rumoured he had become so frivolous with money that once, he got a little inebriated and drove a brand new Lincoln into a motel swimming pool, almost destroying the car. Bill, Dudley and Ernie always drove the latest top-of-the-line cars, and they all enjoyed a hunting lodge Eastern owned at Melrose Lake (Nova Scotia).

The Mingos went frequently to the hunting lodge with their families or family friends and had great times together on the lake. Huge T-bone steaks and lobsters (that no one could finish) were served by the fireplace or out on the screened sundeck, and anyone who played a harmonica, guitar, accordion or sang did so. The kids danced with the adults , or played out in the yard, and the music and laughter lasted well into the wee hours of the morning — long after the children fell exhausted into their bunks. There was a great sense of security about these festive times for the children, knowing the adults were close by, involving them, and laughing and singing long after the kids were sound asleep.

Financial success also allowed the Mingo brothers to provide many of their children with private school education, including boarding schools in Halifax, Windsor and Toronto.

It was common for the owners of Eastern to have huge catered parties, or take a half dozen or more people to dinner and foot the bill. They worked hard and played hard, too. Partying, dancing, singing, drinking and hunting allowed them to blow off steam from the pressures of their work. The Mingos seemed to get together frequently for some kind of festive gathering or another. Bill MacLean was rarely if ever there.

Meanwhile, in 1956, a power development was being constructed in the northern part of Québec. A twelve-mile long tunnel would be blasted through a mountain to redirect a river high enough to make a waterfall to produce energy. The contractor of the project, who, incidentally, owned the New York Yankees at the time, had heard of Eastern's good reputation with prefab buildings. He had a development project to begin soon in Greece and decided to order prefabs from Eastern to help set up his men there. The Greek order was $800,000 worth of prefab camps. The *Financial Post* published an extensive article about Eastern Woodworkers in its June 15, 1957, issue.

By now, Eastern had become so large that Ernie could no longer handle the accounting on his own. Nor could he, Dudley and Bill handle the estimating. Until that year, Ernie and Russell Fitzpatrick, Eastern's chief estimator, had done all the estimating for materials, and Dudley and Bill had done all the estimating for labour. Dudley and Bill also handled all the engineering. Now they hired Fraser Cunningham, a chartered accountant, to look after the books and Frank Mason, an engineer, to look after all construction projects from then on. Frank hired Oral Allan to become chief estimator after Russell left Eastern.

After acquiring yet another large contract in 1958, *The Chronicle-Herald* (Halifax) featured Eastern in an editorial which attributed Eastern with being "one of the most inspiring stories of industrial success in Nova Scotia." It went on to read: "Competing against Central Canadian firms, it has just acquired a $900,000 order from a mining firm for the prefabrication and erection of the necessary buildings for a whole new town in the Quebec wilderness area of Lake Janeen, 260 miles north of Seven Islands [Sept-Îles]. The workmen's housing units, recreation buildings, a church and a hospital will be constructed in sections at the New Glasgow plant and shipped by water this winter to the new mining community." It also quoted Harold who attributed the secret of their success to being "just a case of going out after business and getting it because it won't come to you. And once you get it, work hard to produce economically, to deliver a good product and to establish dependability for your firm."

That same year, Bill was project manager for forty-six houses in St. John's, and Dudley moved with his family to Greenwood, to build 100 houses for the RCAF base there. Construction of Gander continued until 1960 with various superintendents, and Bill, Ernie and Dudley flew to Gander periodically to oversee the projects.

In 1959, Eastern built the Highland View Hospital in Amherst, which Bill supervised, and also bought a prefab industry, Beau Fab, in Ste-Anne-de-Beaupré, Québec — much to the chagrin of Dudley and Ernie. "We didn't want that plant," Ernie says. "We couldn't really afford it, I felt, but Harold had 66% of Eastern and he could do pretty much as he pleased."

The deal had come about because of Doug Sproull, the engineer for Eastern. Doug had been working on a salary and commission basis and doing well — so well he decided to set up business for himself. He had been dating, and soon married, the daughter of the Mayor of Ste-Anne-de-Beaupré and was able to convince his father-in-law to

RCAF Greenwood housing, November, 1958. Eastern erected 100 units for air base personnel at Greenwood, Nova Scotia, in the late 1950s.

The Beau Fab prefabricating plant production facilities, Ste-Anne-de-Beaupré, Québec, circa 1960.

assist him financially in setting up Beau Fab. When he left Eastern, Doug took John Fuller, Eastern's senior draftsman with him. Together, they tried to make Beau Fab work but failed and soon ran into financial difficulty.

Doug came to see Harold in New Glasgow to ask him to buy the business and Harold agreed. Harold reasoned that buying Beau Fab would eliminate any competition in the prefabrication industry. Since Doug and John had worked for Eastern before and were trusted and respected, Harold felt confident in making the two men managers of the company.

Unfortunately, Beau Fab lost $15,000 in the first year alone and $150,000 the next. By 1961, Eastern was forced to fire Doug and John, bring back the useable assets to New Glasgow and sell the rest.

In 1960, Dudley moved to Halifax to construct Mulgrave Park, a $5 million project along Barrington Street. Mulgrave Park would house people displaced by the city's urban redevelopment program, including some from Africville. Africville, a community located at Halifax's Bedford Basin waterfront, would be torn down by the late 1960s.

After Dudley completed Mulgrave Park, he built the nurses residence for the County Hospital in Dartmouth, Nova Scotia. Bill supervised construction of twelve classroom schools in Guysborough and Springhill, Nova Scotia, the West Colchester Rural High School in Bass River, Nova Scotia, and the trade school in Charlottetown.

In 1962, a project of over 200 houses in Summerside had lost nearly $150,000. The superintendent was drinking

---

93

on the job and the weather was some of the worst in the history of the province. Something had to be done about the project to save any further losses. Dudley was forced to complete the job himself.

By now moving was not just a burden for Dudley, it was his major fear. His whole family was suffering. Becoming close friends with people can sometimes take years, but he and his family would just be getting to know people's names, and they theirs, when the Mingos would be shifted off to a new place, to learn new names, new rules, new streets and new games. They were never in one place long enough to know a real sense of security.

At forty-seven Dudley was fed up with packing and unpacking his belongings and having to set up his family in new schools. When he moved to Halifax, he decided this was it! Dudley might have to travel himself but he was not dragging his family through any more moves. Halifax was the centre of commerce and activity for Nova Scotia, and the Maritimes generally, so he felt this was a good place to settle down.

Each Monday morning then, for two and a half years, Dudley waved good-bye to his family, travelled the 180 miles to Summerside to clean up the job someone else was not able to do, and returned home Friday nights to spend the weekend.

Eastern was well-established by now. If one part of the operation suffered losses, profits from the other sectors, particularly contracting which was the most successful, would make up the difference. It consisted of: a sawmill with three million board feet of lumber on hand at any one time, a manufacturing plant for producing cabinets and the like, two dry kilns, a warehouse, an office building with a retail store, a metal workshop — all on Brother street in New Glasgow; a plant at Parkdale in New Glasgow for prefabricating houses and camps; a store in Antigonish,

Partners of Eastern Woodworkers Limited, Eastern Contracting
Limited and Eastern Manufacturing Limited, in 1965: top row, l
to r: President Harold G. Mingo (1911-1987); Secretary-treasurer
and General Manager, Ernest C. Mingo (1917-   ); bottom row, l
to r: Director and Projects Manager Dudley L. Mingo (1914-   );
and Director and Projects Manager J. W. MacLean (1909-1988).

The Chronicle-Herald, *Halifax Nova, Scotia.*

Nova Scotia; a store in Port Hawkesbury, Nova Scotia, opened in 1960; and numerous woodlots. Large contracts were secured in Halifax and in various parts of the Maritimes for schools, banks, churches and the Mill Village (Nova Scotia) Satellite Station; and for Inuit housing units for the Department of Northern Affairs and much more.

Ernie made the papers when he became chairman, then president, of the National Retail Lumberman's Council of Canada in 1961; when he was appointed as one of fifteen delegates to the Canadian Trade Commission in London and to the Advisory Committee of the New Glasgow Branch of Eastern Trust in 1962; and in 1964 when he was appointed chairman of Picord. Several newspapers in 1961 wrote about the history of Eastern, explaining its growth from quarters in a henhouse to one of the most successful businesses in the Maritimes.

Industrial Estates Limited (IEL) represented by Frank Sobey, and Eastern Woodworkers Limited represented by Harold Mingo, entered into an agreement in 1963 to construct a modern manufacturing facility to be built in a convenient spot near the railway tracks on the East River Road in New Glasgow. The company would be called Eastern Manufacturing Limited and would have a 5,000-square foot retail store, a 12,000-square foot warehouse and a modern plant for prefabricating camps and sectional homes.

In 1964, the contracting sector of Eastern Woodworkers Limited was separated from the business again and called Eastern Contracting Limited. And in the following year, Dudley supervised the extension of the biochemistry building for Dalhousie University while Bill completed the foundation for Scott Paper in Abercrombie, Nova Scotia.

The New Glasgow *Evening News* and *The Chronicle-Herald* wrote extensive articles in 1965 to commemorate Eastern Manufacturing on the completion of the East River

*Department heads of Eastern Woodworkers Limited and subsidiaries Eastern Contracting Limited, and Eastern Manufacturing Limited and circa 1965: top row, l. to r., Sales Manager Ray MacDonald, Comptroller Fraser Cunningham, C.A. and Chief engineer Frank Mason, P.Eng.; bottom row, l.to r., Purchasing Agent Carl Mingo, Plant Manager E.A. Sutherland, Eastern Woodworkers Limited and Plant Manager Floyd Mingo, Eastern Manufacturing Limited. (*The Chronicle-Herald, *Halifax Nova, Scotia.)*

Road complex. One explained that "Eastern Woodworkers Limited has reached the position where today it is a leader in the building supply, contracting, and manufacturing fields in this province, and indeed in Atlantic Canada."

The farm boys from the Northumberland Shore had finally made it to the top of their field — something that would have made their mother proud.

The Declining Years
1965-1971

*E*rnie had been the focal point at Eastern, keeping each of the businesses and industries glued together with his personal involvement as accountant and general manager. He wasn't getting any younger, nor was he getting any richer as a shareholder in Eastern. Harold had promised him far more shares in the company than he had ever received. There were still lingering resentments about Gomac among the partners, and because Harold had controlling shares, he could do just about what he pleased.

For years, Ernie had been working long hours, dedicating himself to the success of Eastern despite being a minor shareholder in the businesses and having very little control of where the profits were directed. On the other hand, Harold was taking more and more time off — playing hooky, much as he did from school in his youth. For nearly nine years, the workers at Eastern rarely saw Harold. As a matter of fact, very few workers even knew Harold was president of the company. Yet Harold insisted on continuing to expand the business.

By now Harold was fifty-five, Dudley fifty-two, Ernie

forty-nine and Bill fifty-six. At these ages, partners start slowing down and begin to turn the reins over to younger people — usually their offspring — like the Sobeys and Irvings have done.

But of the five children Harold had, only one of his two sons, Floyd, was old enough to become interested in these male-oriented businesses. Dudley had five daughters; Ernie had two children but only one son, and he was too young to become involved; Bill had two daughters and Carl's children were younger still. Floyd was it; he was the only one at the time to carry on at Eastern. The pressures for Floyd must have been horrendous. He not only had to make it for his father, but also for his uncles and their partner, too. To make matters worse, Harold held control even over his son. Floyd was never able to prove he was his own man to his father.

When the decision was being made to build Eastern Manufacturing, both Ernie and Dudley resisted the project. Ernie knew the plant would demand more time than he was prepared to give and Dudley felt if the venture did proceed, at the very least Eastern Manufacturing should be built in Halifax, not in New Glasgow — a town already saturated with Mingo-owned businesses.

"I held off signing the document to form Eastern Manufacturing for over a year," Ernie says. "I told Harold we just couldn't afford to get into another manufacturing plant. They never really made money. But then one day Marge came to me and said Harold was talking at the dinner table about firing me if I didn't sign. Well, I said to myself, if that's the way I'm going to be treated, I'll do my own thing. That's when I started saying I'd better look after E.C., because she was serious. I signed the document, but from then on I started looking around for opportunities to build apartment buildings and hotels for myself."

So Eastern Manufacturing went ahead on the East River Road in New Glasgow after all, but there were problems from beginning to end. Harold decided to contract the buildings himself, to make sure the project was completed to his strict specifications and standards. An inventor and machinist, not a contractor, Harold lost $30,000 building the plant, warehouse and store.

The buildings were completed, however, and facilities were opened to the public in 1965. The plant for sectional homes lost $75,000 in the first six months of operation. Apparently consumers were not ready for homes that came in two pieces. They thought sectional homes were flimsy and cheap.

Floyd had been running the plant and Ernie fired him. Harold was not happy about the firing and a rift developed between them that was never resolved.

With padlocks on its doors, the Eastern Manufacturing plant shut down for nine months so that Eastern's partners could rethink the situation and decide what to do.

In 1966, the *Daily Commercial News* published an article describing how Eastern had grown "from its small shop with three men to its present widespread operations . . . You will find their prefabricated buildings across Canada: at a shipbuilding and fish processing project at Marystown, Nfld; at a pulp mill construction job at Abercrombie, N.S.; at a power development at Mactaquac, N.B.; at Dept. of Northern Affairs establishments in the Northwest Territories; at mining sites in Quebec's Ungava and in Revelstoke, B.C.; at pulp and paper operations across the country; and, . . . in Greece." And the projects continued. That very year, in Halifax, Eastern built the Saint Mary's University biochemistry and student union buildings and the law building for Dalhousie University. And the following year, Eastern erected the Dartmouth

City Hall, as well as Oceanview Manor in Eastern Passage, and the power plant for Port Hawkesbury.

When the partners reopened the Eastern Manufacturing plant in early 1967, they had geared up to produce mobile homes. The pulp and paper industry, Maritime Tel and Tel and the power companies were turning away from the more expensive prefab camps and houses, to mobile units, because they were more easily transported. Harold felt it would only be a matter of time before consumers would want mobile units for portable hotels, homes and camps and he thought it would be a good bet to be the first to produce them in the region.

Once again, Harold was ahead of the public. Ironically, in a few years when the prospect of building one's own home became too expensive, it would be impossible to meet the demand for sectional or mobile homes. But by then, it would be too late for Eastern. The company was already heading for financial disaster.

Eastern Manufacturing's retail store had accumulated an outrageous accounts receivable in less than three years. "We'd hired this fellow who'd worked at Sears," Ernie says, "and he was ordering carloads of materials. We'd have to have huge sales to get rid of the stuff. I'd get after our accountant, too. It was his responsibility and he wasn't looking after it. Everybody was getting credit and nobody was paying."

For nearly thirty years, Eastern had been considered a great success story — an example of what could be done by those with insight and drive. However, few knew the turmoil involved with operating such a large business. Contracts were secured but whether or not Eastern made money, broke even or went broke over them was a matter of chance. There were so many factors involved in success: the type of men one could get to work; the flow of supplies; weather conditions (the most unpredictable factor) and the age and interest of the principals. Ownership had its rewards but it also had its headaches.

As Eastern Manufacturing lost money, the partners attempted to keep it from collapsing with funds taken primarily from Eastern Contracting. Up until this time both the woodworking and contracting parts of Eastern were fairly secure industries. The woodworking section never made huge profits but it was stable, while the contracting section often made enormous profits. But neither sector could take a constant drain of resources. Eventually both became weaker. By 1968, as signs of Eastern's collapse began to show, the head engineer, Frank Mason, and the accountant, Fraser Cunningham, left Eastern.

Eastern Contracting had an added burden in that bidding was becoming more and more competitive. Ontario companies were underbidding companies in the Maritimes by outrageous amounts, taking tremendous losses in order to penetrate the contracting markets in eastern Canada. Eastern would normally bid on between $30-$40 million worth of contracts each year and secure about $6-$8 million worth. In 1968, Eastern bid on $48 million worth of business and only secured two jobs worth less than $1 million each.

Dineen Construction and Descorti Construction, Upper Canadian companies, were only two of the outside companies able to underbid Maritimes businesses and absorb accumulated losses that could occur. They were huge companies in their own provinces, determined to secure local contracts at any cost in order to gain a foothold in the market. In addition, Harold learned from the manager of Johns Mansville, a gigantic supplier from Montréal, that even though Eastern was Johns Mansville's largest client in eastern Canada, Mansville was charging Ontario companies less for materials because Ontario provided them with more clients and shipping to Ontario was cheaper than to the Maritimes. With Ontario companies underbidding and being able to obtain materials more cheaply, Maritime companies did not stand a chance.

Companies from the Maritimes were finding it more and more difficult to absorb losses. If Eastern had a rough time having to pay accountants, engineers, draftsmen, and two estimators in order to bid on jobs, then it was even harder on smaller companies. Kenny Construction, for instance, underbid an Ontario company (and definitely underbid other Maritime companies) enough to secure contracts in Halifax for the Dalhousie Arts Centre and Fenwick Towers, but went bankrupt over them.

Unions were also a problem for Eastern and always had been. In 1952, Eastern had signed a contract with the carpenters' union (AF of L) but a union organizer for the Steel Workers Union came onto the property.

"This young punk came into my office one day in 1952," Ernie says, "and demanded that we sign with the Steel Workers Union. I said: 'Why would we sign with the steel workers when we've already signed with AF of L?' Well, this punk said if we didn't he'd go out the door right then and there, stick up his hand and pull all our men out. Our men weren't striking. This guy went out into the yard, stuck his hand up and had unemployed miners on the picket line because they were members of the steel workers. It was desperate. One union striking against another. A lot of our men wouldn't go on the picket line but these punks wouldn't let our men work. It got rough. One of our men was going to drive his truck right through their picket line but they let him through. Both plants were closed down in 1952. We had to sign with the steel workers even though we worked with carpenters. It wasn't pleasant. Every year we'd have to negotiate a contract. We'd have to spend many evenings trying to get an agreement.

"By 1966-67," Ernie continues, "we had the highest paid workers in the whole mobile home industry east of Manitoba but there were a lot of young punks in that factory. The other guys were reasonable. But these young guys wanted to be paid the same as Scott Paper. Our finances weren't as good as they had been ten years before. We were starting to go downhill but we had to give them a wage increase anyway. I told them if we gave them this increase we'd go out of business. They didn't care. That was part of the demise of Eastern."

"In 1969," Ernie maintains, "we had a school at Île Madame [Nova Scotia]. Everyone in the labour unions in Cape Breton went out on strike. They weren't striking against us per se; they were striking against the Contractors' Association, but they were out for three months in the summer and that's when you make your money in construction. Then there was the Centennial School in Port Hawkesbury and the power plant. Whenever the men wanted to go hunting or fishing they'd go out on a wildcat strike. Dudley would call me from Cape Breton and I'd have to get into my car, drive to Halifax, talk to a lawyer, get a document and take it to the Department of Labour so they'd give me an order to get the people back to work. That cost money every time."

Dudley adds: "Then, there was an engineer at CMHC who gave us — and all the other contractors around — a lot of trouble in the late '60s. We ended up telling them we wouldn't do any more jobs for them. CMHC was so bad at the time, there was a job in Halifax to build Uniacke Square and Bob Cameron's company was the only one who would put a bid in for CMHC. He had high prices, $16,000 per unit — a massive price we thought — but he got it. Bob made all kinds of money off it because he didn't have any competition to keep his prices down."

Eastern Contracting might still have been able to survive if the profits it was making had not been used to bail out Eastern Manufacturing and some of the other manufacturing facets of the business. But that was not the case. Harold's life was machinery and machinery-built prefabs, mobile homes and sectional homes. He wanted to continue manufacturing whether it was viable or not. He had control and no matter what advice he was given, Harold could do what he wanted and that's exactly what he did. Soon Eastern Contracting was unable to secure the bonds required for bidding. Eastern finished several contracts between 1968 and 1970, but by the fall of 1970, Eastern Contracting had completed its last projects.

In 1969, the partners thought the sale of the Antigonish store would provide the finances required to help maintain Eastern Manufacturing. The Antigonish store was successful, with a hefty profit made each year. Charlie MacCulloch agreed to buy the store but the store burned down two days before the sale was to be officially signed. MacCulloch eventually built his own store on Eastern's old site and set up business for himself in Antigonish. MacCulloch also bought the retail store in New Glasgow, but Eastern was still responsible for the debts the store had accumulated since it had opened

Sectional homes were becoming more popular by this time so Eastern once again jigged for production at Parkdale and Scotia Homes distributed the finished product. The business was more successful than it had ever been, but by now, many pieces of the once huge industry were gone or disintegrating.

In the fall of 1970, Dudley worked on his last job for Eastern Contracting. He could have moved back to New Glasgow to be in charge of the plant on the East River Road (which was producing 100 mobile home units a year distributed by Centennial Trailer Sales), but he could not bear the thought.

From the time he was in his early twenties, Dudley had worked harder than most people ever dreamed of working. He had run from one building to the next, day in day out, making sure each one was properly built. He had given up precious time with his family to dedicate himself to Eastern. During the time he had worked for the company, Dudley had been away from his family for years, seeing them, if he was lucky, on Saturdays or weekends. Added to this were the numerous times he had to pack up his family and take them with him to various towns and villages throughout the Atlantic provinces.

At fifty-six, and bitter, Dudley was not going to reduce himself to being a foreman now. What he got from Eastern he could have gotten from any contracting firm: a large salary and expenses. Eastern had not even provided him with a pension plan or decent bonuses even though his section of the company — contracting — had always made profits, more profits than any other aspect of the business. Gomac Construction had been taken away from him in 1950, his shares had been reduced from 20% to 6% and he had no control over where any of the profits were spent.

Dudley was fed up. He felt he had never let his partners or those at Eastern down but now they were letting him down. As a director and part-owner, he had expected more and not gotten it. He had built monuments during his life. But for the past two years, profits from contracting had been used to bail out non-viable enterprises. Now there wasn't even enough money to bid on jobs. He had to spend time working on piddling things, finishing whatever he could at Eastern Contracting. After all this, he had never even had the luxury of being in one town long enough to develop friends and associates, to make personal investments or to build a decent house for himself as everyone else had. The history of Eastern was not quite over but Dudley was about to abandon ship and run.

When he finished his last job in River Hebert (just outside Amherst) in October 1970, Dudley went to look for work. For the first time in over thirty years he would not be his own boss, but like a broken horse, he did not have the will or energy to start over again for himself.

That same year, 1970, the sawmill was sold in bits and pieces to help cover some of the accounts receivable from the retail store on East River Road. The trailer plant at Eastern Manufacturing reverted to IEL.

Eastern was not going bankrupt nor did it ever go bankrupt, but the commitment needed to overcome the pressures brought on by the various failures within the companies was too much for the principals of Eastern at this stage in their lives. The will was no longer there to try to revive it. Despite this, those at Eastern tried to continue business as long as they could to provide employment for the many loyal employees, some having been with them for thirty years. The plant at Eastern Woodworkers on Brother Street was still operating, as was the plant for sectional homes at Parkdale. But there were too many financial burdens and soon the taxes for such a large but unproductive business became too much.

On February 15, 1971, four months after Dudley had left, and without any warning, representatives of the bank arrived at the offices of Eastern Woodworkers Limited on Brother Street and ordered everyone out. Bill MacLean left with tears in his eyes saying, "After all my years of work, this is what it has come to. Nothing!" Padlocks were put on the doors and the bank now took over Eastern's assets.

Ernie was able to buy some of the equipment with his own private funds two or three days after the bank foreclosed. The receiver sold the store and lot (for building supplies) outside the town of Port Hawkesbury and by March of that year, Ernie and Carl (with two other investors) were able to buy the plant for sectional homes at Parkdale, which they renamed Lanargo Industries Ltd.

"We sold the Royal Bank Building in Gander for $75,000, big trailers and some more stuff to pay off the bank," Dudley says. "They appointed Bill to sell it. The bank hired Doane Raymond and sent their representative. Bill was with him because he knew most of the values of the equipment and assets. When the bank was paid off in November 1971, they were out of there."

"Then we had to deal with the creditors," Ernie says. "Otherwise the creditors would have put us into bankruptcy. I went to a lawyer in Halifax, Robertson was his name. He was an older man, a colonel in the army during the war. Robertson wrote a letter to our creditors telling them, 'If you put Eastern into bankruptcy you won't get anything.' He told them the owners were willing to raise money at the bank to pay them off but it had to be twenty cents on the dollar. So, the creditors accepted this — the big creditors, that is. The smaller creditors we paid in full. That's how we salvaged the assets. Eventually they were sold and there was something left."

In 1971, newspapers throughout the province wrote articles and editorials expressing shock at the closure of Eastern. Some felt government intervention was the ideal solution. If the government bought Eastern, they thought, then the many people who depended on the industry for a living would be able to maintain their jobs. It was even brought before the legislature, but at the time Industry Minister Ralph Fiske said that it was "not viable" for the government to give financial aid. To buy Eastern in its entirety was the preferred choice of the owners, the government and the public at large, but Eastern was one of the largest industries in the Atlantic provinces and prohibitively expensive. Besides, its vast diversity was the result of its unique individuals. Without their winning combination, Eastern could not survive.

What Eastern once was was over.

Epilogue

*A*s the public understood it, Eastern was finished, but selling and settling the remaining assets took many years and many meetings among the owners. Their personal involvement continued for some time.

In August 1975, Eastern's vacant plant on Brother Street in New Glasgow burned down. "The spectacular blaze was visible as far away as Westville," reported one newspaper, "and cast a brilliant orange glow across the sky over New Glasgow." The tower, or boiler which Harold Mingo designed and erected and had been familiar to everyone in New Glasgow as a symbol of production and work for over thirty years, crashed down into the inferno as a crowd of several hundred, clad in housecoats and bedclothes, stood watching in awe and dismay. When the office building at Eastern burned down in 1979, too, there was nothing left of the once prosperous and well-known company.

At the time Eastern closed in 1971, Harold was sixty, Dudley fifty-six, Ernie fifty-four, and Bill sixty-one, not ages to start again from scratch, and not ages to start investing in retirement funds with much hope of accumulating security. But these were resourceful men and each managed in his own way.

Harold, owning 66% of the shares and therefore 66% of the remaining assets, lived a fairly comfortable life after Eastern shut down. A year or two after the closure, Harold invented a septic system which he hoped would revolutionize the restrictive building codes of the construction industry, and in many ways it did. Unfortunately, before Harold could put a patent on the system, a man who was to go into partnership with him opened his own business using Harold's design and information on market potential. After that, Harold lived very much in seclusion in New Glasgow and even more so when he moved to Shubenacadie, Nova Scotia, in 1981. His wife, Marge, had died in 1974 and until his death in March 1987, Harold lived alone, continuing to work with machines and wood, setting up his own workshop in a building in his backyard in Shubenacadie to make cabinets and bookshelves for his children and grandchildren.

Dudley was able to obtain a job within two weeks of leaving Eastern in the fall of 1970. For two years, he worked for a company which paid him minimally. But then, Dineen Construction — ironically one of the companies which helped to put Eastern Contracting out of business by dumping in the Maritimes — made Dudley an offer he couldn't refuse: a better salary than he had ever had at Eastern, a pension plan and bonuses he had never received from his own company.

Happy building the Sheet Harbour Hospital, the extension to the Halifax Infirmary and the Clayton Park Mall, among other projects, Dudley did not retire from Dineen until he was seventy. In part, he felt he could not afford to retire earlier because he only had what he had earned from the time he left Eastern at fifty-six. Ernie gave Dudley twenty-one of his twenty-two shares in Eastern to help him out, but little of the assets were left after taxes, expenses and everyone else's shares had been distributed.

Yet Dudley has maintained a fairly good standard of living despite everything. He is eighty-one now, in excellent health, walks four miles a day, owns his own property with income, and a cottage on the Northumberland Shore. His family has become so extended, it is hard to keep track of all their names. He may not live as high profile a life as he once did when an owner of Eastern, and he would rather not move back to New Glasgow where there are too many ghosts, but Dudley is content with his life. He loves his wife, Bernice, whom he has been married to for fifty-six years. And he is proud to say that even in his mid and late seventies, companies, including the government, were calling to ask him to work for them. Instead of accepting these offers, Dudley enjoys his retirement, maintaining his properties, visiting family and dancing whenever there is an opportunity.

Ernie faired best of anyone. When he was under Harold's threat to fire him in the early 1960s, Ernie began investing in enterprises for himself and never again invested in anything which did not provide him with 51% of the shares. Now he owns the Wandlyn Motels in Port Hawkesbury and Antigonish, the Silver Dart Lodge in Baddeck, Nova Scotia, a blueberry industry, a senior citizens complex in New Glasgow, a cottage at Chance Harbour, a condo in Florida and much more. By the time Eastern had gone under, Ernie was well enough off (although he gleaned most of his wealth after Eastern's demise) not to be adversely affected financially by the closure. Because he was secure, he was able (as mentioned before) to buy the Parkdale Plant from the receiver and set up his brother, Carl, in the sectional homes business. Carl, unfortunately, died of cancer at the age of sixty-one in 1985. Ernie also had two bouts with bowel cancer but he is as healthy as anyone at seventy-nine, is still a going concern investing in new enterprises with his son, Donald, and spending four to six months of the year in Florida with his wife, Eve.

Bill MacLean got the worst of it when Eastern closed in 1971. He was sixty-one. Bill had very few shares in the company and his health was not good (being a diabetic and having had a heart attack in 1967). He worked for several years in the New Glasgow area with Fraser and Hoyt after Eastern's closure and he lived pretty much as he had before: quietly with his family. Bill was no slouch when it came to dollars and cents, however. He had always lived fairly frugally, even at Eastern's peak, so although he did not have a pension or many investments, Bill was well enough off to live comfortably until his death in 1988, at the age of seventy-nine. Marion, his wife, died two months after he did.

* * * * * *

Today, Dudley and Ernie remain best friends. They do not, however, punch each other in the nose any more. Instead, they visit frequently, drink rum, tell stories, go to dances together with their spouses, and recently worked together on Ernie's senior citizens' complex in New Glasgow. Their postures are straight, their eyes bright, their skin tanned, their minds sharp and they still dress better than most. They are two very distinguished looking men — still a winning combination at seventy-nine and eighty-one.

Appendix

CONTRACTS COMPLETED BY EASTERN

Every attempt has been made to include all contracts Eastern completed, and to be accurate with the names of those who worked as superintendents on projects for Eastern. Please note: from 1957, Frank Mason was the chief engineer on all Eastern contracts.

Chart headings:
PROJ M=project manager, SUPER= superintendent.

Abbreviations:

ASR=airport surveillance radar
Bldg=building
CBC=Canadian Broadcasting Corporation,
CNR=Canadian National Railways
Dal=Dalhousie University
DND=Department of National Defence,

DOT=Department of Transpotation
KLM=Royal Dutch Airlines
Mt A=Mount Allison University
NB=New Brunswick
Nfld=Newfoundland
NS=Nova Scotia
PAR=perimeter acquisition radar

PEI=Prince Edward Island
Pq=Province of Québec
RCAF=Royal Canadian Air Force
RCMP=Royal Canadian Mounted Police
SMU=Saint Mary's University
SUB= student union building

DATE	CONTRACT	PROJ M	SUPER	AMOUNT
'39	Refrigerator parts for cold storage, restaurant furnishings and remodelling Canso, NS			
'40	Millwork, Sydney			

116

Year	Description			Amount
'40	Millwork, Sydney Airport, NS			$ 75,000
'41	Millwork, Stanley Airport, PEI			
'41	Millwork and hangar doors, Summerside Airport, PEI			
'41	250 prefabricated houses	D.L. Mingo	D.L. Mingo	
'41	100 houses, Amherst, NS	D.L. Mingo	D.L. Mingo	
'41	3 staff houses and commissary, New Glasgow, NS	J.W. MacLean	D.L. Mingo	
'41-43	400 houses, Pictou, NS	J.W. MacLean	D.L. Mingo	
'41	Recreation Center, Pictou, NS	J.W. MacLean		
'41	3 staff houses and commissary, Pictou, NS	J.W. MacLean	D.L. Mingo	
'42	136 houses, New Glasgow, NS	D.L. Mingo		
'43-45	175 cargo barges	D.L. Mingo H.G. Mingo	E. Sutherland A. Arbuckle D.L. Mingo	
'47-49	50 houses, Woodstock, NB	J.W. MacLean	E. Sutherland	$ 240,000
	50 houses, New Glasgow, NS	D.L. Mingo	El Cameron	$ 265,000

117

DATE	CONTRACT	PROJ M	SUPER	AMOUNT
	29 houses, Charlotte-town, PEI	J.W. MacLean	E. Sutherland	$ 165,000
	35 houses, Amherst, NS	J.W. MacLean	Don Gould	$ 195,000
	25 houses, Stellarton, NS	D.L. Mingo		$ 135,000
'49-50	100 houses, Chatham, NB	J.W. MacLean	Don Gould	$ 635,474
'49-50	66 houses, Halifax, NS	D.L. Mingo	Alex Cameron	$ 454,171
'50-51	105 houses, Summerside, PEI	D.L. Mingo	Alex Cameron / Bill Kilner	$ 602,433
'50-51	Stadium, New Glasgow, NS	J.W. MacLean	F. McDougall	$ 172,300
'50-51	24 houses, Coverdale, NB	J.W. MacLean	Don Gould	$ 162,496
'51-52	Unit supply and construction engineering bldg, Summerside, PEI	J.W. MacLean	F. McDougall / Lester Mingo	$ 453,299
'51-52	100 houses, Shearwater, NS	D.L. Mingo	Alex Cameron / Don Gould	$ 855,764
'51-53	570 units army huts	H.G. Mingo	Bill Damery	$ 5,182,180
'52-53	Combined maintenance and storage garage, Shearwater, NS	J.W. MacLean	Don Gould	$ 304,645

Year	Description			Amount
'52-53	100 houses, St. John's, Nfld	D.L. Mingo	Bill Kilner Bill Noel	$ 1,105,360
'52-53	50 houses, Gander, Nfld	J.W. MacLean	F. McDougall	$ 529,111
'52-53	50 houses, Gander, Nfld	J.W. MacLean	F. McDougall	$ 540,359
'54-55	30 houses, Gander, Nfld	J.W. MacLean	F. McDougall	$ 324,884
'55	50 houses, Cornwallis, NS	J.W. MacLean	Don Gould	$ 446,108
'54-55	180-man barracks, Halifax, NS	D.L. Mingo	R.MacPherson	$ 428,790
'54	Government bldg, Moncton, NB	J.W. MacLean	Burke	$ 171,700
'54	Transmitter bldg,power house, PAR and ASR bldg, and others, Gander, Nfld	J.W. MacLean	F. McDougall	$ 228,876
'54	School, Spryfield, NS	D.L. Mingo		$ 92,900
'54	Greenwood School, Pictou County, NS	J.W. MacLean	Bill Kilner	$ 46,600
'54	Resthouse, CNR, Havre Boucher, NS	J.W. MacLean	Elliott	$ 36,977
'55	Royal Bank bldg, Gander, Nfld	D.L. Mingo	F. McDougall	$ 42,500
'55	54 single family housing units, Gander, Nfld	D.L. Mingo	F. McDougall	$ 594,320

DATE	CONTRACT	PROJ M	SUPER	AMOUNT
'55-57	Federal public bldg, Grand Falls, Nfld	D.L. Mingo	Burtie Buckler	$ 230,977
'55	Garage, Hickman Motors, Gander, Nfld	D.L. Mingo	Jake Dike	$ 86,957
'55	11 housing units, Gander, Nfld	D.L. Mingo	Jim Broderick	
'55	Mining camp, Canadian British Aluminum, Baie Comeau, PQ	D.L. Mingo		
'55-57	116 housing units, DOT, Gander, Nfld	D.L. Mingo	H. Ramsey	$ 1,169,297
'55	High school extension, Grand Falls, Nfld	D.L. Mingo	Alex Cameron	$ 8,000
'55	Married quarters, RCMP, Grand Falls, Nfld	D.L. Mingo	Alex Cameron	$ 27,190
'55	Cohen Store, Grand Falls, Nfld	D.L. Mingo	F. MacKinnon	$ 82,442
'55	Studio, CBC, Gander, Nfld	D.L. Mingo	Jake Dike	$ 46,300
'55	Anglican church, Gander, Nfld	D.L. Mingo	Jim Broderick	$ 8,622
'55	Transmitter, CBC, Grand Falls, Nfld	D.L. Mingo	Alex Cameron	$ 60,000

Year	Project	Architect	Contractor	Amount
'55-56	Married quarters #2, RCMP Grand Falls, Nfld	D.L. Mingo	Alex Cameron	$ 28,690
'55-56	Federal bldg, Grand Falls, Nfld	D.L. Mingo	George Noel	$ 350,000
'55-57	Leahy Cinema, Gander, Nfld	D.L. Mingo	Jake Dike	$ 130,921
'55-57	T. Eaton bldg, Gander, Nfld	D.L. Mingo	Jake Dike	$ 239,035
'55-57	Eaton's warehouse, Gander, Nfld	D.L. Mingo	H. Ramsey	$ 42,000
'55-57	Service station, Imperial Oil Gander, Nfld	D.L. Mingo	Jake Dike	$ 26,000
'55-57	St. Michael's School, Grand Falls, Nfld	D.L. Mingo	Dan O'Hanley	$ 397,205
'55-57	107 houses, DND, St. Margaret's, NB	J.W. MacLean	Don Gould	$ 1,259,557
'56-57	215 houses, DND, Camp Gagetown, NB	J.W. MacLean	Alex Cameron	$ 2,187,080
'56-57	Stage #1 school, St. Margaret's, NB	J.W. MacLean	Don Gould	$ 177,889
'56-57	St. Joseph's School, Gander, Nfld	D.L. Mingo	Jake Dike	$ 359,027
'56-57	Amalgamated school, Gander, Nfld	D.L. Mingo	Ches Baxter	$ 654,672

DATE	CONTRACT	PROJ M	SUPER	AMOUNT
'56	3 houses, KLM, Gander, Nfld	D.L. Mingo	Jim Broderick	$ 43,500
'56	133 houses, Camp Gagetown, NB	J.W. MacLean	Alex Cameron	$ 1,423,112
'56	Physics and engineering bldg, Mt A, Sackville, NB	J.W. MacLean	F. MacKinnon	$ 368,929
'57	Stores bldg, radio station, Gander, Nfld	D.L. Mingo	H. Ramsey	$ 1,990
'57	19 classroom school, Camp Gagetown, NB	J.W. MacLean	Burtie Buckler	$ 506,403
'57	96 houses, Gander, Nfld	D.L. Mingo	H. Ramsey	$ 1,154,955
'57	D.U. Smith building, Amherst, NS	J.W. MacLean		$ 75,000
'57	St. Joseph's Church basement, Gander, Nfld	D.L. Mingo	Jim Broderick	$ 46,190
'57	Consolidated high school, Judique, NS	Frank Mason	Floyd Mingo	$ 180,018
'57	MacGregor House, Gander, Nfld	D.L. Mingo	H. Ramsey	$ 13,850
'58-59	46 houses, St. John's, Nfld	J.W. MacLean	Alex Cameron	$ 598,000
'58-59	100 houses, RCAF Greenwood, NS	D.L. Mingo	Don Gould	$ 1,120,000
'59	School, Bridgetown, NS	D.L. Mingo	Don Gould	$ 250,000

Year	Project			Amount
'59	5 houses, Middleton, NS	D.L. Mingo	Don Gould	$ 75,000
'59	Philips Electric bldg, Dartmouth, NS	Frank Mason	Ches Baxter	$ 250,000
'59	Highland View Hospital, Amherst, NS	J.W. MacLean	Dave Savoie	$ 350,000
'59	Installation for Cartier Mining, PQ	Frank Mason	Dave Savoie	$ 500,000
'59-60	Warehouse and office, NS. Liquor Commission, Halifax, NS	Frank Mason	Alex Cameron	$ 320,000
'60	North West Presbyterian Church, Halifax, NS	J.W. MacLean	John McLellan	$ 130,000
'60	Addition, West King's District High, Auburn, NS	D.L. Mingo	Bill Kilner	$ 225,000
'60	9 room school extension, Amherst, NS	J.W. MacLean	John McLellan	$ 280,000
'60	Penitentiary bldg, Springhill, NS	J.W. MacLean		$ 295,000
'60	12 classroom school, Guysboro, NS	J.W. MacLean	Floyd Mingo	$ 240,000
'61	2 transmitter bldgs, DOT, Canso, NS	Frank Mason		$ 90,000
'61	West Colchester Rural High, Bass River, NS	J.W. MacLean	Burtie Buckler	$ 350,000

DATE	CONTRACT	PROJ M	SUPER	AMOUNT
'61	12 classroom school, Springhill, NS	J.W. MacLean	John McLellan	$ 480,000
'61	Armament bldg, Greenwood, NS	Frank Mason	Bill Kilner	$ 210,000
'61	8 room elementary school, Dartmouth, NS	Frank Mason	Dave Savoie	$ 360,000
'60-61	350 Units, Mulgrave Park, Halifax, NS	D.L. Mingo	Ches Baxter Hudson Ramsey Emit Cameron Bill Kilner Don Gould	$ 5,000,000
'61	Research barns, Agriculture College, Truro, NS	J.W. MacLean	Joe LeFresne	$ 160,000
'61	Trade school, Sydney, NS	J.W. MacLean	Ches Baxter	$ 530,000
'62	100 houses, Saint John, NB	J.W. MacLean	Dick Goad	$ 1,350,000
'62	200 units, Summerside, PEI	D.L. Mingo	H. Ramsey	$ 2,400,000
'62	Men's residence, Mt A, Sackville, NB	J.W. MacLean	Ches Baxter	$ 330,000
'62-63	Trade school, stage #2 and #3, Charlottetown, PEI	J.W. MacLean	Dave Savoie	$ 520,000

Year	Project			Amount
'63	Nurses' residence, NS County Hospital, Dartmouth, NS	D.L. Mingo	Emit Cameron	$ 480,000
'63	Extension, High School, New Glasgow, NS	Frank Mason	Burtie Buckler	$ 225,000
'63	Main branch, Royal Bank, Charlottetown, PEI	Frank Mason	Ches Baxter	$ 310,000
'63	Royal Bank, Port Hawkesbury, NS	Frank Mason	Burtie Buckler	$ 180,000
'63	Anglican church, Port Hawkesbury, NS	Frank Mason	Burtie Buckler	$ 150,000
'63	United Church, Pictou, NS	J.W. MacLean	Floyd Mingo	$ 175,000
'63	Junior High, Westville, NS	Frank Mason	Joe LeFresne	$ 325,000
'64	Temporary bldg, Clairtone, Stellarton, NS	J.W. MacLean	Don Gough	$ 250,000
'64	High school, West Pictou, NS	Frank Mason	Burtie Buckler	$ 375,000
'64	Vocational school, Stellarton, NS	Frank Mason	Floyd Mingo	$ 325,000
'64	Maritime Moving & Storage, Halifax, NS	D.L. Mingo	Burtie Buckler	$ 220,000
'64	Men's residence, Dal, Halifax, NS	D.L. Mingo	Burtie Buckler	$ 435,000

DATE	CONTRACT	PROJ M	SUPER	AMOUNT
'64-65	Satellite Station, Mill Village, NS	D.L. Mingo, Frank Mason	Ches Baxter, Bill Kilner	$ 650,000
'64	Elementary school, Sackville, NS	D.L. Mingo	John McLellan	$ 295,000
'65	Biochemistry bldg extension, Dal, Halifax, NS	D.L. Mingo	Bill Kilner	$ 800,000
'65	Foundation, Scott Paper, Abercrombie, NS	J.W. MacLean	H. Ramsey	$ 500,000
'65	Port Hawkesbury United, Port Hawkesbury, NS	Frank Mason	John McLellan	$ 210,000
'65	Junior high school, Westville, NS	Frank Mason		$ 500,000
'65	Sutherland Memorial Hospital, Pictou, NS	Frank Mason	Ches Baxter	$ 320,000
'65	Warehouse, Scott Paper, Abercrombie, NS	J.W. MacLean	H. Ramsey	$ 350,000
'65	Brawmore, School Extension, Antigonish, NS	Frank Mason		$ 180,000
'65	Gymnasium, NS Teacher's College, Truro, NS	Frank Mason	John McLellan	$ 240,000
'65	Windsor Hall, Ladies Dorm, Mt A, Sackville, NB	Frank Mason	Ches Baxter	$ 345,000

Year	Project, Location	Engineer	Contact	Amount
'66	Biochemistry bldg, SMU, Halifax, NS	D.L. Mingo	Joe Armstrong	$ 560,000
'66	SUB, phase #1, SMU, Halifax, NS	D.L. Mingo	Burtie Buckler	$ 150,000
'66	Lighthouse and 2 houses, County Island, NS	Frank Mason	M. McPhee	$ 90,000
'66	Law bldg, Dal, Halifax, NS	D.L. Mingo		$ 1,400,000
'67	Esso Service Centre, Halifax, NS	D.L. Mingo	Ted Kirk	$ 315,000
'67	City Hall, Dartmouth, NS	Frank Mason	Ches Baxter	$ 1,000,000
'67	School extension, D'Ecousse, NS	D.L. Mingo / Frank Mason	MacKenzie	$ 135,000
'67	Esso Service Centre, Economy, NS	J.W. MacLean	Joe LeFresne	$ 140,000
'67	Oceanview Manor, Eastern Passage, NS	J.W. MacLean	H. Ramsey / Dave Savoie	$ 2,000,000
'67-68	Power plant, phase #1, Port Hawkesbury, NS	D.L. Mingo	M. MacPhee	$ 800,000
'67-68	Junior high, Port Hawkesbury, NS	D.L. Mingo / Frank Mason	Ches Baxter	$ 380,000

DATE	CONTRACT	PROJ M	SUPER	AMOUNT
'68-69	High school extension, Isle Madame, NS	D.L. Mingo	MacKenzie	$ 1,115,000
'68-69	High school extension, Barrington Passage, NS	Frank Mason	H. Ramsey	$ 295,000
'69	100 trailers, Gulf Oil, Port Hawkesbury, NS	D.L. Mingo	A. MacDonald	$ 650,000
'69	30 trailers, Pitts Construction (for wharf), Port Hawkesbury, NS	D.L. Mingo	A. MacDonald	$ 210,000
'70	Elementary school, River John, NS	J.W. MacLean	Joe LeFresne	$ 280,000
'70	High school, extension and renovation, River Hebert, NS	D.L. Mingo	Joe Armstrong	$ 310,000